Christ in All of Scripture

A 52-WEEK JOURNEY OF DISCOVERING JESUS
ON EVERY PAGE OF THE BIBLE

Volume Four

This study belongs to:

_____

THE DAILY GRACE CO.®

Christ in All of Scripture: A 52-Week Journey of Discovering Jesus on Every Page of the Bible | Volume 4
Copyright © 2024 by The Daily Grace Co.®
Spring, Texas. All rights reserved.

Unless otherwise noted, all Scripture quotations are taken from the Christian Standard Bible®, Copyright © 2020 by Holman Bible Publishers. Used by permission. Christian Standard Bible® and CSB® are federally registered trademarks of Holman Bible Publishers.

Supplemental material: pages 12, 14–17, 190–191, and 199–201. Copyright © 2019 by The Daily Grace Co.®

Supplemental material: pages 8–10, 13, 188–189, and 193–198. Copyright © 2024 by The Daily Grace Co.®

The extras on pages 73 and 149 were originally published in *The Bible Handbook: A Book-by-Book Guide to the Entire Bible*. Copyright © 2020, 2024 by The Daily Grace Co.®

The Daily Grace Co.® exists to equip disciples to know and love God and His Word by creating beautiful, theologically rich, and accessible resources so that God may be glorified and the gospel made known.

Designed in the United States of America and printed in China.

In seeing how He is present throughout the whole Bible, your love for Jesus and for His Word will grow.

Table of Contents

INTRODUCTION

How to Use This Resource 8
Study Suggestions 12
How to Study the Bible 14
Timeline of Scripture 16

WEEK FORTY 19
WEEK FORTY-ONE 35
WEEK FORTY-TWO 47
WEEK FORTY-THREE 59
WEEK FORTY-FOUR 75
WEEK FORTY-FIVE 89
WEEK FORTY-SIX 101
WEEK FORTY-SEVEN 113
WEEK FORTY-EIGHT 125
WEEK FORTY-NINE 137
WEEK FIFTY 151
WEEK FIFTY-ONE 163
WEEK FIFTY-TWO 175

EXTRAS

God as the Shepherd of His People 33
God's *Hesed* Love
   in the Book of Hosea 73
Prophecies of the Holy Spirit 86
Messianic Passages in Zechariah 149
Appendix A:
   How to See Christ
     in All of Scripture 188
Appendix B:
   The Attributes of God 190
Appendix C:
   Annotation Examples and Tips 193
Appendix D:
   The Metanarrative of Scripture 199
What is the Gospel? 200

Introduction to
Christ in All of Scripture | Volume 4

You've made it to *Christ in All of Scripture: A 52-Week Journey of Discovering Jesus on Every Page of the Bible | Volume 4*!

As you continue in your study, remember that the Old Testament and New Testament tell one story, and they are far more intertwined than we sometimes realize. As we saw from the beginning of the first volume, that story begins in the Old Testament, and it contains numerous threads that run throughout and find their resolution in the New Testament. Because of this, we cannot fully appreciate the New Testament without also appreciating the Old—and vice versa.

And standing at the center of this one story that unites both testaments is Jesus Christ. He Himself is the main character and climax of the story that began in the Old Testament. For that reason, we can appropriately say that Jesus Christ is present in *all* of Scripture, not just a quarter of it.

Of course, it's easy to *say* that Jesus is in all of Scripture. But the study you hold in your hands will help you *see* it. And our prayer is that in seeing how He is present throughout the whole Bible, your love for Jesus and for His Word will grow.

> Jesus is present in *all* of Scripture, not just a quarter of it.

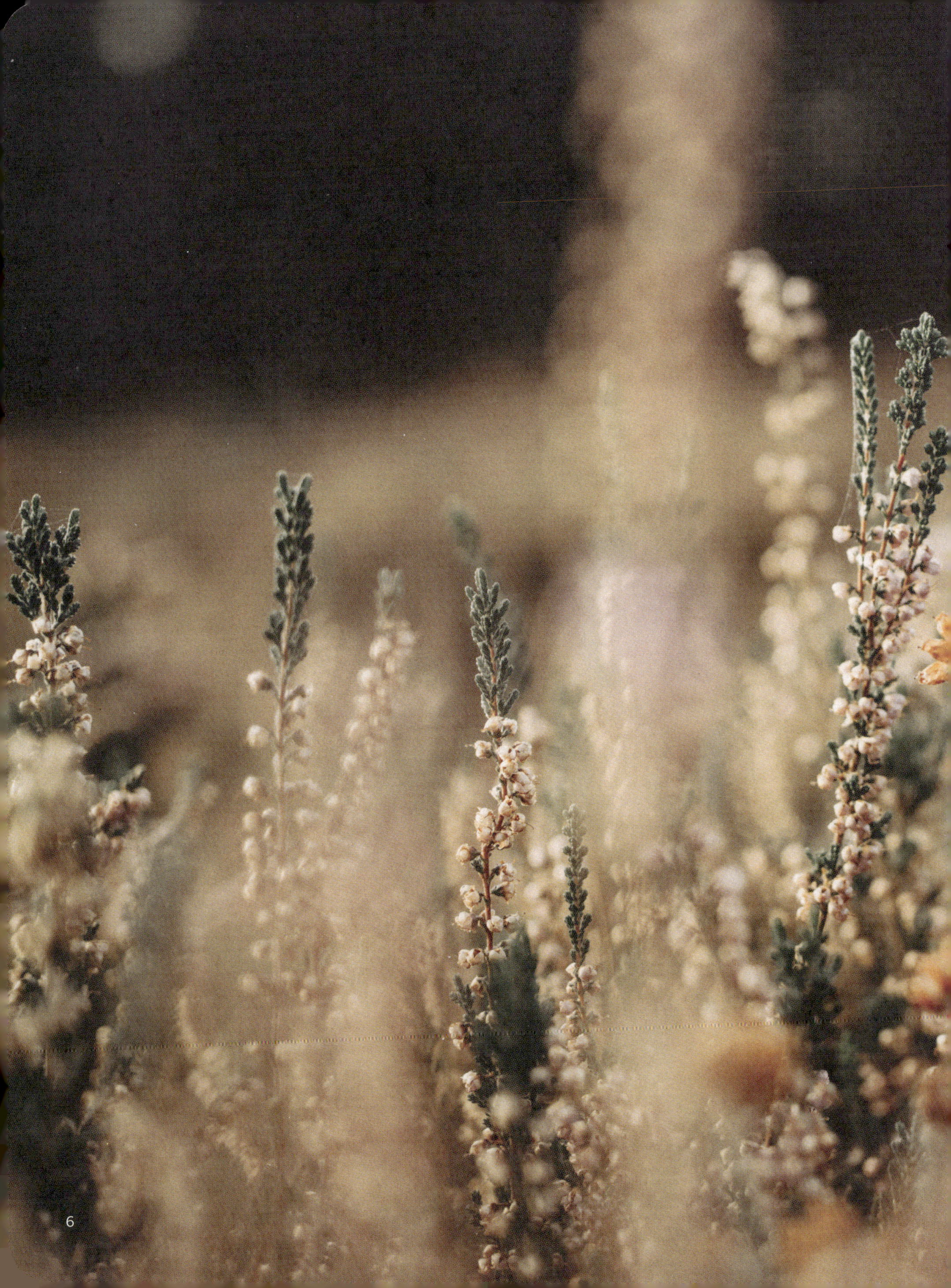

As you continue in this yearlong journey, remember that the goal of this study is not perfection but growth in your understanding of God's Word.

How to Use This Resource

As our journey continues, this section provides reminders of some practical considerations that will help you make the most of this study.

IN THIS STUDY

This study is the fourth and final volume in the *Christ in All of Scripture* study set from The Daily Grace Co.® Each volume covers roughly one quarter, or thirteen weeks, of content. And together, these four volumes were designed to be completed over the course of one calendar year—from January 1 through December 31.

> NOTE:
> Visit www.thedailygraceco.com to purchase the other three volumes in this study set (Volumes 1, 2, and 3).

Over the course of this year—just as we did in the first three volumes—we will continue walking through passages from most of the books of the Old Testament, showing how these passages ultimately point to Jesus. In this way, we will discover how Christ is truly present on every page and in every passage of Scripture.

WEEKLY RHYTHMS

The main content of this study starts in Week 40. There are five days of content for each week, so most readers will likely find it helpful to complete the study content on Mondays through Fridays. Then, the weekends can be used to catch up on any missed study days or to reflect on what you learned.

Each week in this volume contains the following elements:

Weekly Introduction
Each week will begin with a short introduction that will share the Old Testament and New Testament passages of Scripture we will study that week.

Days 1 and 3: "Mark it Up"
On Days 1 and 3, you will be asked to repetitively read and annotate our two weekly passages. If the idea of annotation seems overwhelming to you—perhaps something you have not done since high school English class—do not fret! We will provide helpful prompts to guide you along the way. You can also find some annotation examples on pages 193–198.

These study days might initially seem quite short, especially compared to past Bible studies you may have completed, but we encourage you to make the most of this step! The observations you make on Days 1 and 3—through the highlights, underlines, and notes you write in the margins—will guide the rest of your progress throughout the week.

> *For annotation examples, as well as other helpful tips and tools for completing this study, see the Appendix, starting on page 187.*

Additionally, if you come across a prompt that challenges you or leaves you with more questions than answers, that's okay! You may find it helpful to look at the surrounding context of that passage (i.e., the verses or chapters that come just before and just after it). And at times, you may simply jot down your questions to come back to later in the week.

Days 2 and 4: "Go Deeper" + "Make the Christ Connection"
On Days 2 and 4, you will find commentary that helps further explain and connect that week's passages of Scripture, as well as some questions that will help you more deeply consider what you have read and make connections of your own. We suggest you begin these days by rereading the passages. Then, give yourself plenty of time to read the commentary and answer the questions as you go deeper into each passage.

Day 5: "Live It Out"
Finally, the week will end with some intentional time to consider how you might apply what you have learned. This is an important step that will help you move from head knowledge to heart knowledge and then to actionable steps to live out the truths you have learned. We suggest you start Day 5 by reading that week's main passages of Scripture once more and then setting aside some time to pray and walk through the provided application questions as you consider how God might be calling you to respond.

Week 52: Conclusion Week
Finally, this study will end with a conclusion week. Similar to the prep week that kicked off the study in Volume 1, this conclusion week is not broken up into individual study days. Instead, it is designed for you to go through at your own pace as you pray and reflect on all that you have learned over the course of this yearlong study.

Whether this is your first time completing a Bible study or you have been studying God's Word for decades, the unique weekly format of this study may still feel new and perhaps even challenging at first. If that's the case for you, don't forget to give yourself grace through the process and remember that God has not left you to study His Word on your own. If you are a believer, His Spirit dwells within you and will guide you as you approach Scripture.

AS YOU CONTINUE

Ready to keep going? As you continue in this yearlong journey, remember that the goal of this study is not perfection but growth in your understanding of God's Word. In other words, we do not expect you to annotate every passage or answer every question perfectly. Instead—day by day, week by week, and volume by volume—we pray that you would progressively grow in your ability to see Christ in all of Scripture. And as you do, we pray that you will grow to love Him and His Word more.

Jesus is the main character of the story. He is the One to whom all of Scripture points. And so, let us seek to magnify Him as we embark on the remaining weeks of study. To Him be the glory!

Day by day, week by week, and volume by volume—we pray that you would progressively grow in your ability to see Christ in all of Scripture.

Study Suggestions

We believe that the Bible is true, trustworthy, and timeless and that it is vitally important for all believers. These study suggestions are intended to help you more effectively study Scripture as you seek to know and love God through His Word.

SUGGESTED STUDY TOOLS

- ☐ Bible
- ☐ Journal to write notes or prayers
- ☐ Pens, colored pencils, and highlighters
- ☐ Dictionary to look up unfamiliar words

Did you know that there is a podcast that goes along with this study?

A YEAR IN THE BIBLE
WITH DAILY GRACE®

Check out season 4 of *A Year in the Bible with Daily Grace* for encouragement as you complete this study—available wherever you listen to podcasts.

How to Study the Bible

The Inductive Method provides tools for deeper and more intentional Bible study. This study will guide you through the three steps of the Inductive Method listed below—equipping you to observe, interpret, and apply two passages of Scripture each week. In addition, the questions listed under each of the steps below can be used to aid your study of the weekly passages.

Weekly rhythm: On Days 1 and 3 of each week, we recommend referring to the "observation and comprehension" step and key question. On Days 2 and 4, we recommend following the "interpretation" step and key question. And on Day 5, we recommend referencing the "application" step and key question.

Observation & Comprehension

KEY QUESTION: WHAT DOES THE TEXT SAY?

After reading the daily Scripture in its entirety at least once, begin working with smaller portions of the Scripture. Read a passage of Scripture repetitively, and then mark the following items in the text:

- Key or repeated words and ideas
- Key themes
- Transition words (e.g., therefore, but, because, if/then, likewise, etc.)
- Lists
- Comparisons and contrasts
- Commands
- Unfamiliar words (look these up in a dictionary)
- Questions you have about the text

Interpretation

KEY QUESTION: WHAT DOES THE TEXT MEAN?

Once you have annotated the text, work through the following steps to help you interpret its meaning:

- Read the passage in other versions for a better understanding of the text.
- Read cross-references to help interpret Scripture with Scripture.
- Paraphrase or summarize the passage to check for understanding.
- Identify how the text reflects the metanarrative of Scripture, which is the story of creation, fall, redemption, and restoration.
- Read trustworthy commentaries if you need further insight into the meaning of the passage.

Application
KEY QUESTION: HOW SHOULD THE TRUTH OF THIS PASSAGE CHANGE ME?

Bible study is not merely an intellectual pursuit. The truths about God, ourselves, and the gospel that we discover in Scripture should produce transformation in our hearts and lives. Answer the following questions and prompts as you consider what you have learned in your study:

- What attributes of God's character are revealed in the passage?
- Consider places where the text directly states the character of God, as well as how His character is revealed through His words and actions.
- What do I learn about myself in light of who God is?
- Consider how you fall short of God's character, how the text reveals your sin nature, and what it says about your new identity in Christ.
- How should this truth change me?
- A passage of Scripture may contain direct commands telling us what to do or warnings about sins to avoid in order to help us grow in holiness. Other times, our application flows out of seeing ourselves in light of God's character. As we pray and reflect on how God is calling us to change in light of His Word, we should be asking questions like, "How should I pray for God to change my heart?" and "What practical steps can I take toward cultivating habits of holiness?"

Timeline of Scripture

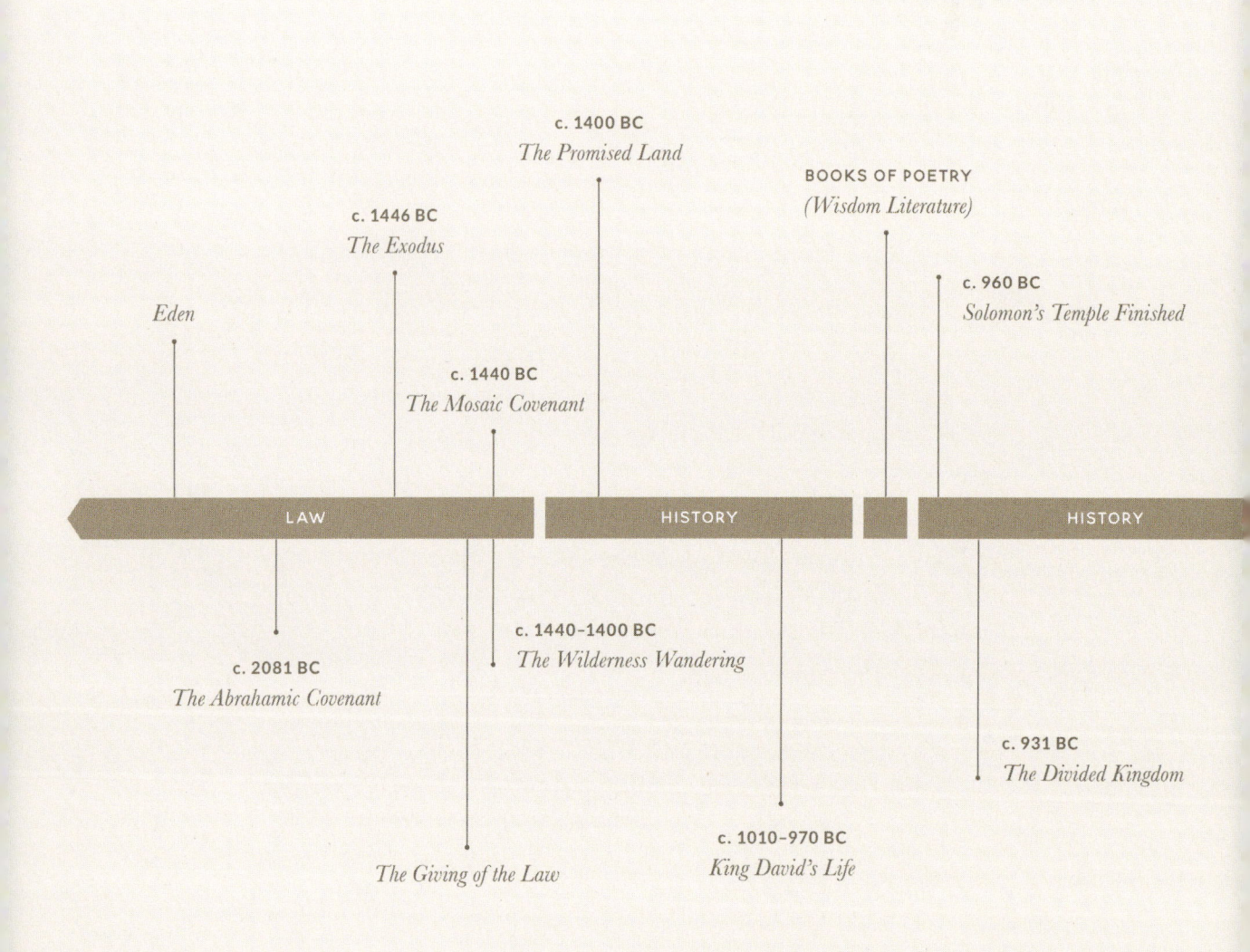

Eden

c. 2081 BC
The Abrahamic Covenant

LAW

c. 1446 BC
The Exodus

The Giving of the Law

c. 1440 BC
The Mosaic Covenant

c. 1440–1400 BC
The Wilderness Wandering

c. 1400 BC
The Promised Land

HISTORY

c. 1010–970 BC
King David's Life

BOOKS OF POETRY
(Wisdom Literature)

c. 960 BC
Solomon's Temple Finished

HISTORY

c. 931 BC
The Divided Kingdom

c. 722 BC
Israel Exiled to Assyria

c. 4 BC
The Birth of Jesus

c. AD 30–62
Acts of the Disciples

c. 537 BC
Judah's Exiles Return Home

c. AD 34
Paul Converted

c. AD 70
Second Temple Destroyed

c. 515 BC
Second Temple Built

| PROPHETS | GOSPELS | HISTORY | EPISTLES |

c. 587 BC
Solomon's Temple Destroyed and the Final Exile to Babylon

c. AD 30
Jesus's Death

The Letters

The Intertestamental Period

Timeline of Scripture / 17

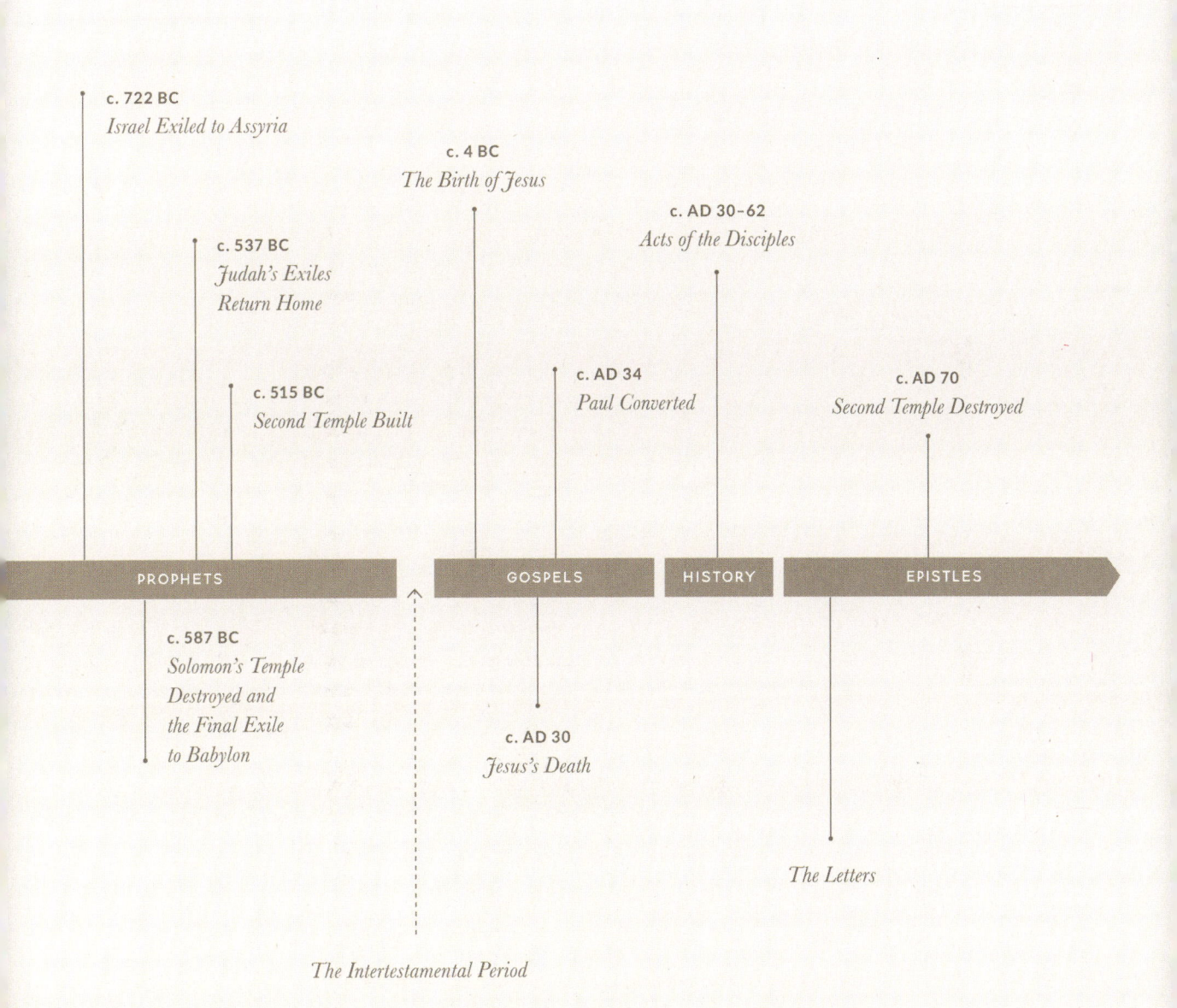

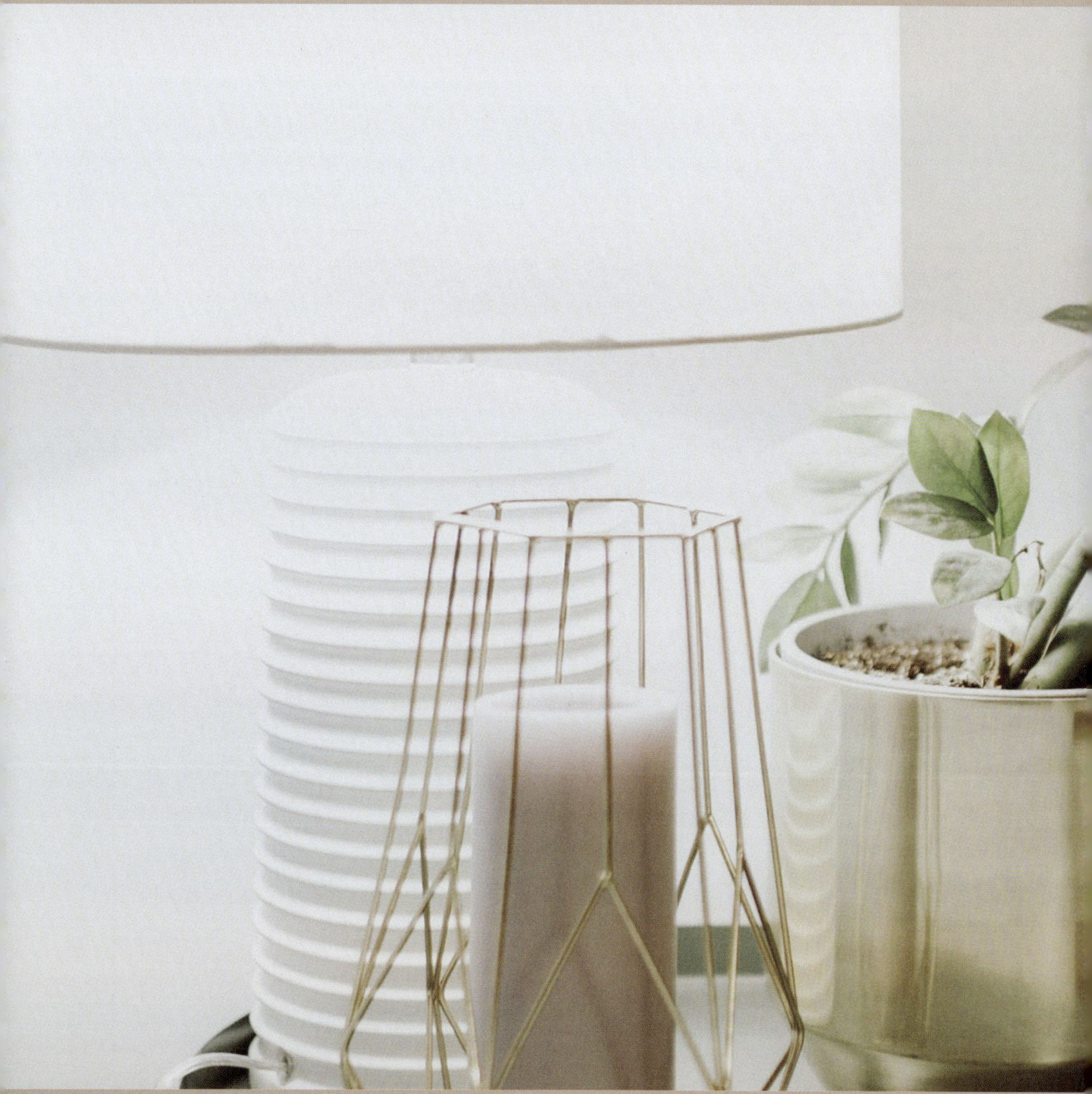

WEEK 40

Introduction

This week, we will read Ezekiel 34:7–16 and John 10:11–15, learning how God's promise to shepherd His people is ultimately fulfilled in Jesus Christ—the Good Shepherd. In response, you will be encouraged to follow and trust Jesus as He leads you and cares for you.

God shepherds His people and seeks to save the lost.

Mark it Up: Old Testament Passage

Today, we will begin the week by looking at Ezekiel 34:7–16. As we do, we will see how God shepherds His people and seeks to save the lost. Read Ezekiel 34:7–16 two or three times and annotate, or mark up, the text as you read. For tips and examples on annotating, see pages 188–199.

Highlight any words or phrases that point to Christ.

Make note of any attributes of God seen in the text.

Circle every instance of the words "I will." List out what God promises to do.

Underline the word "shepherd" when it appears in the passage.

EZEKIEL 34:7–16

⁷ "'Therefore, you shepherds, hear the word of the Lord. ⁸ As I live—this is the declaration of the Lord God—because my flock, lacking a shepherd, has become prey and food for every wild animal, and because my shepherds do not search for my flock, and because the shepherds feed themselves rather than my flock, ⁹ therefore, you shepherds, hear the word of the Lord!

¹⁰ "'This is what the Lord God says: Look, I am against the shepherds. I will demand my flock from them and prevent them from shepherding the flock. The shepherds will no longer feed themselves, for I will rescue my flock from their mouths so that they will not be food for them.

¹¹ "'For this is what the Lord God says: See, I myself will search for my flock and look for them. ¹² As a shepherd looks for his sheep on the day he is among his scattered flock, so I will look for my flock. I will rescue them from all the places where they have been scattered on a day of clouds and total darkness. ¹³ I will bring them out from the peoples, gather them from the countries, and bring them to their own soil. I will shepherd them on the mountains of Israel, in the ravines, and in all the inhabited places of the land. ¹⁴ I will tend them in good pasture, and their grazing place will be on Israel's lofty mountains. There they will lie down in a good grazing place; they will feed in rich pasture on the mountains of Israel. ¹⁵ I will tend my flock and let them lie down. This is the declaration of the Lord God. ¹⁶ I will seek the lost, bring back the strays, bandage the injured, and strengthen the weak, but I will destroy the fat and the strong. I will shepherd them with justice.'"

Go Deeper

> Read Ezekiel 34:7–16.

The Israelites were once a people who followed and obeyed the Lord. While they were not perfect in their obedience, the people of Israel generally thrived when led by godly leaders such as Moses, Joshua, and David (Exodus 24:6–7, Joshua 1:16–17, Psalm 78:72). But as we have seen, all of this changed after David's son, Solomon, died. Israel had one king after another who turned away from the Lord to worship the gods of the nations around them. While we do see some kings who sought to obey God and lead the people well, most were wicked and disobedient, leading the Israelites to become wicked and disobedient as well.

By the time we come to the book of Ezekiel, we see that the Israelites have become a wayward people. Their consistent disobedience to the Lord has resulted in them being exiled. While this exile is due to Israel's wayward worship, God desires to restore His people and bring them back to their land. It is in Ezekiel 34:11–16 that we see God's promise of restoration through His promise to shepherd His people.

But before God speaks these words of promise and hope to His people, He declares judgment on Israel's leaders (Ezekiel 34:7–10). God uses Ezekiel to prophesy against Israel's shepherds, or leaders, who were supposed to be spiritually caring for Israel and looking after them. But these leaders have done the opposite of caring for Israel, for they have fed themselves instead of Israel. They have left Israel vulnerable to attack from other nations. They have not searched for the ones who have been scattered by the nations. All these actions show how these people have utterly failed to shepherd God's people.

> Why is God's judgment upon these leaders fair?

Because these leaders have failed to properly shepherd Israel, God's judgment is coming upon them. However, God also promises to be the people's Shepherd. He will look for and rescue the lost. He will gather them together and bring them back to their home. He will give them food, rest, and healing. And unlike the failed shepherds (Ezekiel 34:2–4), God will shepherd the people with justice (Ezekiel 34:16). He will not allow the Israelites to be mistreated or allow those who stand against them to go unpunished. All of God's promises in this passage show God's heart and immense care for His people. God desires to seek and save the lost, and it is by His actions alone that He will find, save, and restore Israel.

> What do God's actions and promises in this passage teach you about His character?

God declares Himself to be Israel's Shepherd, but we also see Him promise another shepherd. Later, in Ezekiel 34:23–24, God promises to raise up a shepherd who will lead and guide Israel: "I will establish over them one shepherd, my servant David, and he will shepherd them. He will tend them himself and will be their shepherd. I, the Lord, will be their God, and my servant David will be a prince among them. I, the Lord, have spoken." Though God will fulfill His promises to shepherd Israel, His promise will ultimately be fulfilled by One who will come from David's line, a David-like figure who will lead God's people better than any leader who has come before. This person, the Messiah, will be the true Shepherd of God's people.

> Spend some time in prayer, thanking God for His desire to seek and save the lost and for providing rest and healing in Himself.

Mark it Up: New Testament Passage

Today, we will read the New Testament passage of John 10:11–15 and learn how God's promise to shepherd His people is ultimately fulfilled in Jesus Christ, the true and better Shepherd. Read the passage two or three times and annotate, or mark up, the text as you read. For tips and examples on annotating, see pages 188–199.

Highlight any words or phrases that point to Christ.

Make note of any attributes of God seen in the text.

Underline what Jesus calls Himself in verses 11 and 14.

Circle the words "my own" where they appear in the passage.

Highlight in another color what Jesus says He does for His sheep, according to verse 15.

God's promise to shepherd His people is ultimately fulfilled in Jesus Christ, the true and better Shepherd.

JOHN 10:11–15

[11] "I am the good shepherd. The good shepherd lays down his life for the sheep.

[12] The hired hand, since he is not the shepherd and doesn't own the sheep,

leaves them and runs away when he sees a wolf coming. The wolf then snatches

and scatters them. [13] This happens because he is a hired hand and doesn't care

about the sheep. [14] I am the good shepherd. I know my own,

and my own know me, [15] just as the Father knows me,

and I know the Father. I lay down my life for the sheep."

Make the Christ Connection

> Read Ezekiel 34:7–16 and John 10:11–15.

In Ezekiel 34, God had promised to shepherd His people and raise up a shepherd for them, and in John 10:11–15, we see this promise fulfilled. In John 10, Jesus has been confronting the Pharisees by demonstrating their spiritual blindness. The Pharisees believe they are righteous because of their strict obedience to God's law. But their pride blinds them from seeing the truth. They are not leading the people as they should, for they are judgmental and legalistic, weighing the people down with burdens rather than humbly encouraging them in their worship of God (Matthew 23:4). Once again, God's people have unfit leaders.

However, while the Pharisees have failed to shepherd God's people as they ought to, Jesus shows Himself to be the true and better Shepherd for His people in John 10:11–15. Unlike a hired hand who leaves the sheep vulnerable to attack and does not care for them, Jesus cares so much for His sheep that He lays His life down for them. He is the Good Shepherd who does not leave His people wandering astray.

> Read John 10:17–18. How does the truth that Jesus willingly laid down His life for you humble you?

Jesus's words in this passage show that He is the fulfillment of the Shepherd whom God promised to raise up in Ezekiel 34. In fact, Jesus is the fulfillment of all that God promised in Ezekiel 34 when it comes to shepherding His people. Jesus is the One who seeks and saves the lost. He does not stand idly by as people stumble around in the darkness of sin. He does not watch from a distance as people wander away from God and His truth. Instead, He calls the lost to Himself, inviting them to experience salvation through Him. He makes a way for sinners to come into God's fold, or His family, and be intimately known by their Shepherd (John 10:14). Jesus makes all of this possible through His death and resurrection as He laid His life down on the cross in order to save the lost. Because of Jesus, we are found and forgiven.

> Read Matthew 18:10–14. How do you see the truths about who Jesus is and what Jesus does, as described in John 10:11–15, reflected in Matthew 18:10–14?

In a similar way, 1 Peter 2:24–25 also boasts of these truths about our salvation in Christ our Shepherd. Peter writes, "He himself bore our sins in his body on the tree; so that, having died to sins, we might live for righteousness. By his wounds you have been healed. For you were like sheep going astray, but you have now returned to the Shepherd and Overseer of your souls." Jesus's sacrifice on the cross saves us from being lost in the darkness of our sin. His forgiveness cleanses our sin and binds up our brokenness. And the salvation He gives grants us eternal life in Him. As followers of Christ, we have the sure hope that our Good Shepherd keeps us safe in His hands, and nothing can remove us from His loving care (John 10:28–29). We belong to our Shepherd, and He belongs to us, forever.

> Read Psalm 23 and reflect on how God has fulfilled these shepherdly qualities and actions through Christ. Then, pray a prayer of gratitude to the Lord.

Live it Out

Read Ezekiel 34:7–16 and John 10:11–15.

Jesus is the true and better Shepherd, our Good Shepherd, who laid His life down for us on the cross. Such a precious truth should lead us to praise Jesus every day for saving us and bringing us into His family. It is a gift to belong to God's family, and we should treasure this gift.

One of the ways we can treasure this gift is by responding to our salvation and position with the Lord through obedience to Christ. We should follow our Shepherd above all else, listening to His voice as we seek to be obedient to Him (John 10:16, 27). It can be so easy to listen to other voices that call out to us, promising us life and satisfaction. But our Good Shepherd's voice matters the most, for it is in Him that true life and satisfaction are found.

Because Jesus is our ultimate Shepherd, we should see Him as the One who ultimately cares and provides for us. When we are in need, we can look to Jesus and trust in Him, knowing that He takes care of us. And when earthly shepherds fail, we can look to and trust in our Good Shepherd, knowing that He is the One who is ultimately in control and keeps us safe within His hands (John 10:28–29).

We also have hope that when Jesus returns, justice will be executed upon earthly shepherds who have led others astray. As we follow Jesus, we cling tightly to the words of Revelation 7:17: "For the Lamb who is at the center of the throne will shepherd them; he will guide them to springs of the waters of life, and God will wipe away every tear from their eyes." Jesus, our Good Shepherd, will guide us all of our days and bring us safely home.

Reflect on this week's verses as you answer the following questions.

What does it look like to listen to Jesus's voice above all others?

How can you rely on Jesus to help you and care for you when you walk through difficult times?

How does the truth that Jesus keeps you safe and leads you into eternity give you hope in the present?

We belong to our Shepherd,
and He belongs to us, forever.

God as the Shepherd of His People

GOD AS SHEPHERD

The L{ord} is my shepherd;
I have what I need.
He lets me lie down in green pastures;
he leads me beside quiet waters.
Psalm 23:1–2

The L{ord} is the strength of his people;
he is a stronghold of salvation
for his anointed.
Save your people, bless
your possession,
shepherd them, and
carry them forever.
Psalm 28:8–9

See, the Lord G{od} comes
with strength,
and his power establishes his rule.
His wages are with him,
and his reward accompanies him.
He protects his flock like a shepherd;
he gathers the lambs in his arms
and carries them in the
fold of his garment.
He gently leads those that are nursing.
Isaiah 40:10–11

For this is what the Lord G{od}
says: See, I myself will search for
my flock and look for them.
Ezekiel 34:11

CHRIST AS SHEPHERD

And you, Bethlehem, in
the land of Judah,
are by no means least among
the rulers of Judah:
Because out of you will come a ruler
who will shepherd my people Israel.
Matthew 2:6

I am the good shepherd. The
good shepherd lays down
his life for the sheep.
John 10:11

For the Lamb who is at the
center of the throne
will shepherd them;
he will guide them to springs
of the waters of life,
and God will wipe away every
tear from their eyes.
Revelation 7:17

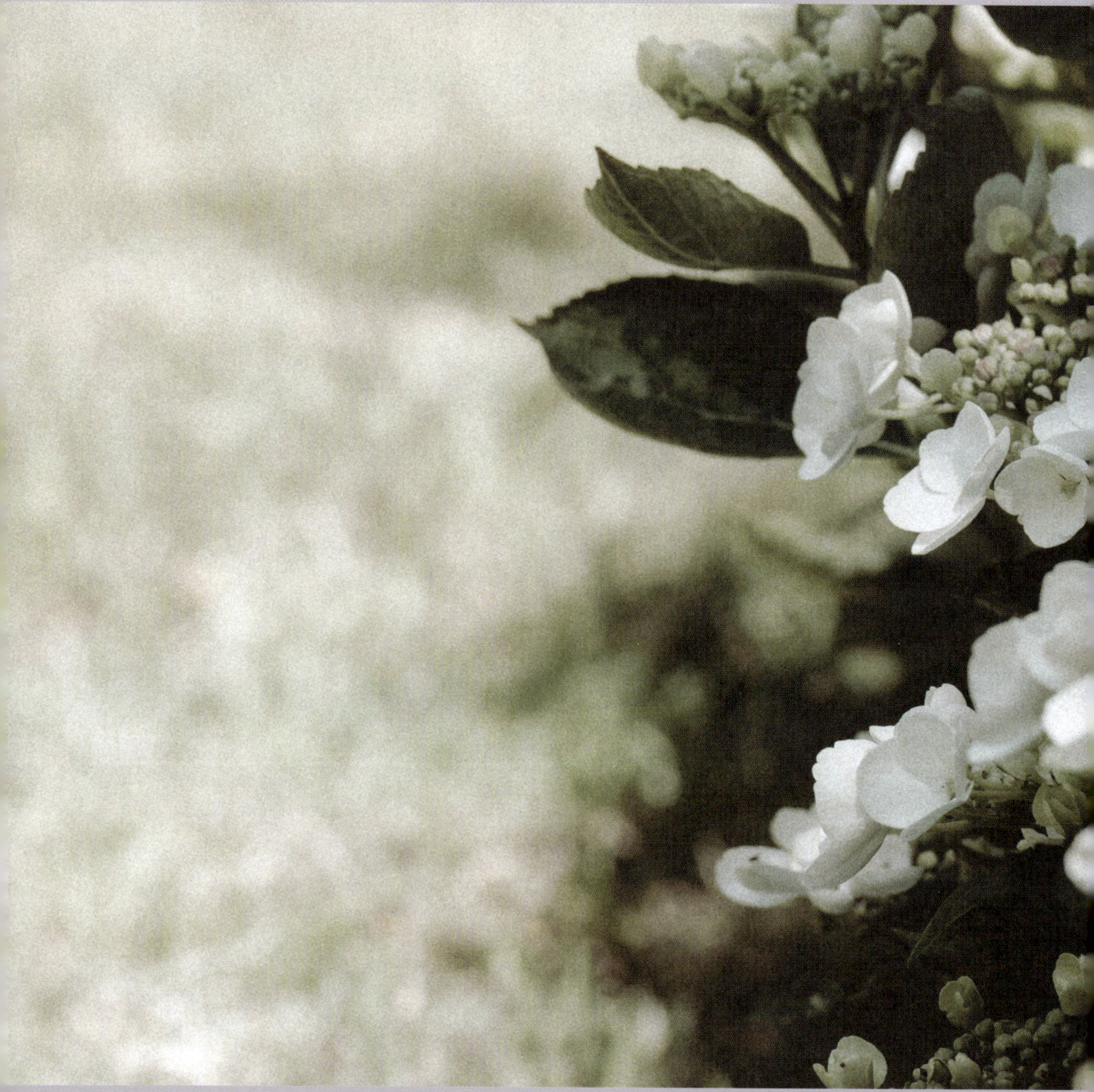

WEEK 41

Introduction

This week, we will trace the work of the Holy Spirit through Ezekiel 36:26–27 and Romans 8:1–4, learning that Jesus sends His Spirit who enables us to walk in God's ways. In response, we will not only be challenged to examine our own hearts, but we will also be encouraged to rejoice in Jesus's fulfillment of the Law and the Spirit's work in us through our faith in Christ.

W41 / D1

Mark it Up: Old Testament Passage

Today, we will study Ezekiel 36:26–27 and explore God's promise to give His people new hearts. Read the passage two or three times and annotate, or mark up, the text as you read. For tips and examples on annotating, see pages 188–199.

Highlight any words or phrases that point to Christ.

Make note of any attributes of God seen in the text.

Circle the phrase "I will." Who is speaking here?

Underline the word "new." What is being made new in this passage?

Highlight in another color any references to God's actions in the text.

Draw a box around the word "Spirit" in verse 27.
What is the role of the Holy Spirit in this passage?

EZEKIEL 36:26–27

²⁶ I will give you a new heart and put a new spirit within you; I will remove your heart of stone and give you a heart of flesh. ²⁷ I will place my Spirit within you and cause you to follow my statutes and carefully observe my ordinances.

Go Deeper

> Read Ezekiel 36:26–27.

Ezekiel was a prophet appointed to his role during the time of Judah's exile to Babylon. At this point in redemptive history, the people of Judah have been banished from their homeland because of their persistent trespasses against God. Like their ancestors before them, God's people are caught in a cycle of sin—rebelling continually against Him. Even their leaders are corrupt, dismissing God's commands and encouraging others to do the same. To get their attention and call them to repentance, God has Ezekiel perform multiple signs—signs that are profound and yet may seem strange to us. For example, in Ezekiel 12:3–6, God commands Ezekiel to dramatically act out Judah's exile as a warning of their fate.

But, like the prophets before and after him, Ezekiel also carries a message of hope. He prophesies to the people of Judah of a time that is coming when they will have brand-new hearts. The type of transformation Ezekiel describes is a change of will—a change of inclination. He is prophesying a coming change in the ways the people think, the reasons they act, and the desires they have.

> Why were the people of Judah in need of new hearts? Why are we, too, in need of new hearts?

The prophet Jeremiah, who prophesied in the years before Judah's exile and Ezekiel's subsequent ministry, called the heart wicked, deceitful, and desperately sick (Jeremiah 17:9, see also NLT and ESV). His words have been proven true throughout all of human history as we have exhibited our inability to obey God time and time again. The hearts of the people of Judah—and the hearts of all men and women—are in need of change. Ezekiel promises that God will not just reform the hearts of His people but that He will give them completely new hearts—hearts that will love what God loves and hate what He hates.

Through the prophet Ezekiel, God promises a time of restoration for His people. Instead of having hearts that desire evil, they will have hearts that desire justice. Instead of having hearts that are selfish and idolatrous, they will have hearts that are devoted to the Lord.

> Read Deuteronomy 30:6–8. According to this passage, what type of heart and spirit does God desire from His people?

In Deuteronomy 30:6–8, God describes the heart of loyalty and love that He desires from His people. Ezekiel's words give us a glimpse into what it might be like to have such a heart of devotion. Yet because the people of Judah have proven that they cannot produce obedience within themselves, they need Someone to redeem them. God would one day redeem and restore His people through His Son Jesus, giving them soft and malleable hearts made of flesh in place of their hearts made of stone. He would send His Spirit to dwell in them, working in them and enabling them to obey God's laws.

> How—and through whom—will God's people be restored? Pray a prayer of thanksgiving for God's mercy exhibited through Ezekiel's prophecy.

Mark it Up: New Testament Passage

Today, we will see that Jesus sends the Spirit, who enables us to walk in God's ways. Read Romans 8:1–4 two or three times and annotate, or mark up, the text as you read. For tips and examples on annotating, see pages 188–199.

Highlight any words or phrases that point to Christ.

Make note of any attributes of God seen in the text.

Circle the word "Spirit." What is the role of the Holy Spirit in this passage?

Draw a box around who is described as being free from condemnation in Romans 8:1. Why is this?

ROMANS 8:1-4

¹ Therefore, there is now no condemnation for those in Christ Jesus, ² because the law of the Spirit of life in Christ Jesus has set you free from the law of sin and death.

³ For what the law could not do since it was weakened by the flesh, God did. He condemned sin in the flesh by sending his own Son in the likeness of sinful flesh as a sin offering, ⁴ in order that the law's requirement would be fulfilled in us who do not walk according to the flesh but according to the Spirit.

Make the Christ Connection

Read Romans 8:1–4.

Ezekiel prophesied of a time coming when God's people would have new hearts that would be able to love and obey Him. In the past, the Law had acted as a guardian, helping God's people to see and understand God's character and know how to walk in holiness (Galatians 3:24). However, the Law could not make them obedient. In fact, the Law revealed just how wicked and rebellious the human heart is as the people of Israel demonstrated their inability to obey it. What they needed was not modification of their behavior but completely new hearts. But Jesus met the Law's requirements, and those requirements have now been fulfilled in us who have been given the Spirit, who helps us to walk in God's ways.

> How does faith in Jesus impart a new heart and a new spirit in the lives of those who place their trust in Him?

Jesus, in His perfect obedience and righteousness, fulfilled the Law. What we could not do, God did by sending His Son to live a perfect life and die the death that we deserved as lawbreakers. Those who place their faith in Christ are now delivered from the condemnation that was wrought by sin and disobedience (Romans 8:1–2). In Christ, we also receive the Spirit, who gives us a new heart—a heart that desires to love and obey God (Romans 8:3–4).

> How does having a new heart in Christ change the way we react and relate to God and His Word?

Through His life, death, and resurrection, Jesus enacts the New Covenant that was prophesied by Ezekiel, and we are able to enter into it by faith in Him. No longer are the hearts of men in bondage to sin and ruled by their flesh. Galatians 5:22–25 teaches us that, by the Spirit, we produce fruit that is consistent with the Spirit—fruit that pleases God—as we yield to the Spirit's leading. Where our hearts were once wicked, deceitful, and desperately sick, we now have hearts that desire to please God.

Jesus is the promised Messiah who gives His people soft and malleable hearts made of flesh in place of their hearts made of stone that did not love or obey God (Ezekiel 36:26). Those who place their faith in Jesus are living proof of Ezekiel's prophecy as the Spirit of God enables them to follow God's statutes and obey His commands (Ezekiel 36:27). Christ's obedience enables obedience in the heart of every believer who puts their trust in Jesus for salvation, thus receiving His Holy Spirit.

> Pause and pray, thanking God for the new heart He has given you.
> Ask Him to help you be led by the Spirit.

Live it Out

> Read Ezekiel 36:26–27 and Romans 8:1–4.

Ezekiel's prophecy gave us a glimpse of God's vision for a people who would love Him in return. Romans 8:1–4 shows us that Jesus fulfilled this prophecy by offering His life for us. Those who place their faith in Christ's sacrifice receive the Holy Spirit as a down payment on a future heavenly reality (Ephesians 1:14) and as a means to lead lives of faithfulness to God here and now. Because of Jesus, we are no longer condemned to the eternal exile wrought by sin.

The Spirit of God living within us animates our obedience. Just like the ancient Israelites who stumbled, fell, and self-destructed through their pattern of sin, we were bound for an eternity apart from God. But praise God for the gift of His Spirit who gives us new hearts and new life. Though we will still wrestle with sin, we are no longer bound by sin's curse. By the Spirit, we have the desire and ability to obey God. And through our desires and actions, we see the evidence of God's Spirit within us.

Though we are not saved by works — the things that we do — our works flow out of our hearts (James 2:18). If our hearts have been transformed by the Spirit, we will desire to obey God. We will begin to act like Jesus. When we sin, we will experience conviction and the desire to repent. The Holy Spirit in us radically transforms our life, and the longer we walk with Jesus, the more we are sanctified — made more like Christ.

Reflect on this week's verses as you answer the following questions.

> Read Galatians 5:22–24. What is the evidence of the Holy Spirit's work in us?

Has your heart been transformed by the Holy Spirit? What evidence of the Spirit's work is present in your day-to-day life?

Write a prayer of gratitude, thanking God for the Spirit who does for us what we could have never done for ourselves by enabling us to love and obey God.

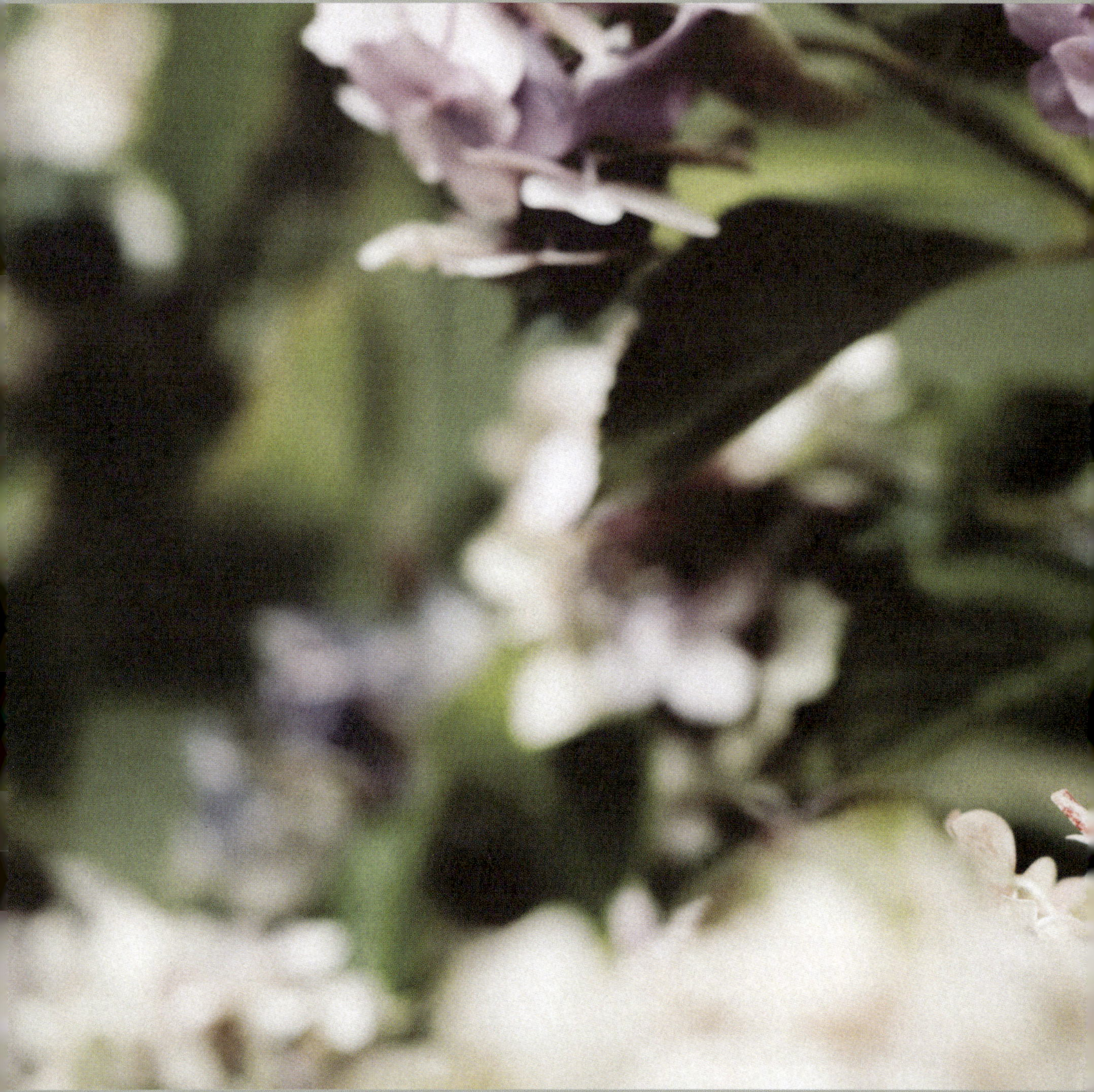

WEEK 42

Introduction

This week, we will read Daniel 7:13–14 and Matthew 24:29–31 as we learn that Jesus is the Son of Man who will return to establish His kingdom. In response, you will be encouraged to hope in Jesus, whose return is certain.

Mark it Up: Old Testament Passage

Today, we will read Daniel 7:13–14 and learn of God's promise to send One who will reign over an eternal kingdom. Read the passage two or three times and annotate, or mark up, the text as you read. For tips and examples on annotating, see pages 188–199.

Highlight any words or phrases that point to Christ.

Make note of any attributes of God seen in the text.

According to verse 13, who appears, and whom does He approach?

Underline the description of how this person appears in verse 13.

Draw a box around what this person receives in verse 14.

Highlight in another color how this person's kingdom is described.

DANIEL 7:13-14

¹³ I continued watching in the night visions,

and suddenly one like a son of man

was coming with the clouds of heaven.

He approached the Ancient of Days

and was escorted before him.

¹⁴ He was given dominion

and glory and a kingdom,

so that those of every people,

nation, and language

should serve him.

His dominion is an everlasting dominion

that will not pass away,

and his kingdom is one

that will not be destroyed.

Go Deeper

> Read Daniel 7:13–14.

When you see or hear the word "apocalyptic," what do you envision? You might think of the end of the world or a time of mass destruction. Usually, the term "apocalyptic" evokes a feeling of fear. But in the Bible, apocalyptic literature and passages are meant to give us hope rather than fear. In reference to Scripture, this word refers to a divine revelation from God of what is unknown to us. It is like getting to peek behind a curtain and glimpse events taking place behind the scenes.

In Daniel 7, Daniel receives an apocalyptic revelation from the Lord. As this chapter begins, Daniel's vision seems terrible at first. But then, what Daniel sees in verses 13–14 brings peace instead of fear, as these verses describe a divine Man whose kingdom will be better than any of the kingdoms of this earth.

The events in the book of Daniel take place while Daniel and his fellow Israelites are exiled in Babylon. At this time, Babylon is a powerful nation. But in Daniel 7, Daniel receives a revelation regarding other nations—nations seemingly more powerful than Babylon. In verses 1–8, Daniel sees four beasts coming from the sea, and he is told in verse 17 that these beasts symbolize nations that will bring chaos and destruction. The description of these beasts is horrifying, and we would likely be terrified to receive visions of them, just as Daniel is (Daniel 7:15). But Daniel sees more that brings hope to this fearful vision.

First, Daniel sees someone who he refers to as "the Ancient of Days" (verses 9–10). He is described as powerful and glorious, as He sits on a flaming throne and has thousands of people who serve him. But then, a man comes on the scene—a man Daniel describes as someone "like a son of man" (verse 13). "Son of man" is a phrase in the Bible that refers to a human. It is a human man who appears, but it is clear that He is divine, for He comes on the clouds of heaven (Psalm 68:4, 104:3–4, Isaiah 19:1). This person is able to approach the Ancient of Days and be escorted before Him. His authority is confirmed as He receives glory and a kingdom that will be eternal and unshakeable (verse 14).

> Read Daniel 7:11–12. What happens to the other kingdoms in these verses? How does the kingdom described in verse 14 compare to these kingdoms?

This revelation changes the context of the vision of the horrible beasts Daniel has seen. Though the four nations that the beasts represent are powerful kingdoms, the Son of Man's kingdom will be greater. Not only this, but unlike the kingdoms of this earth, the Son of Man's kingdom will be everlasting. Those kingdoms that Daniel sees will eventually crumble, but the Son of Man's kingdom will remain.

> Consider what is being revealed in Daniel 7:13–14. How do you think these words bring Daniel hope?

While the visions that Daniel sees in Daniel 7 may seem confusing and frightening, the hope nestled within them allows Daniel to have peace even amid the destruction that is to come. The Ancient of Days—God—is on the throne. He has the utmost authority over these terrible nations and will defeat them. And one day, a powerful divine Man, whose kingdom reigns supreme, will appear.

> Consider the truth that God holds the ultimate authority over all the kingdoms of this earth. Spend some time in prayer, praising God for His sovereignty.

Mark it Up: New Testament Passage

As we come to our New Testament passage today, we will read Matthew 24:29–31 and learn how Jesus is the fulfillment of the Son of Man who will one day come in glory. Read the passage two or three times and annotate, or mark up, the text as you read. For tips and examples on annotating, see pages 188–199.

> Highlight any words or phrases that point to Christ.

> Make note of any attributes of God seen in the text.

> Draw a box around every occurrence of the words "Son of Man" in the passage.

> Highlight in another color the description in verse 30 of how the Son of Man will appear.

> Circle what the Son of Man will do, according to verse 31.

Jesus is the fulfillment of the Son of Man who will one day come in glory.

MATTHEW 24:29–31

²⁹ "Immediately after the distress of those days, the sun will be darkened, and the moon will not shed its light; the stars will fall from the sky, and the powers of the heavens will be shaken. ³⁰ Then the sign of the Son of Man will appear in the sky, and then all the peoples of the earth will mourn; and they will see the Son of Man coming on the clouds of heaven with power and great glory.

³¹ He will send out his angels with a loud trumpet, and they will gather his elect from the four winds, from one end of the sky to the other."

Make the Christ Connection

> Read Daniel 7:13–14 and Matthew 24:29–31.

As long as we live on this side of eternity, we will experience nations rising and falling. However, we still have hope. God is more powerful than the kingdoms of this earth, and His kingdom will one day be the only kingdom that will stand. When Jesus returns, God's kingdom will be fully realized, and God's people will experience what it is like to live under God's glorious reign forever. In Matthew 24:29–31, we receive a glimpse of Jesus's return and how such events point back to Daniel 7.

Matthew 24:29–31 takes place after Jesus predicts a time of destruction that will involve great distress and despair. But Jesus also promises that, after this time, the Son of Man will appear in power and glory. Jesus states that the coming of this Son of Man will involve mourning. This means that there will be people who grieve because they recognize that judgment is about to come upon them. Yet, while there will be fear and mourning for some, there will be great hope for His people, the elect. Jesus describes how the Son of Man will gather his elect from all over the earth, bringing them to Himself.

> How does Jesus's Second Coming bring comfort to us today?

The Son of Man described by Jesus in Matthew 24:29–31 is Himself. Jesus defeated sin and death through His death on the cross and resurrection, revealing how God's kingdom is more powerful than the kingdom of darkness. Jesus also ascended on the clouds after His resurrection and will appear again in the same way (Matthew 24:30, Acts 1:9–11). While Jesus's past and future actions reveal Him to be the Son of Man, Jesus also refers to Himself as the Son of Man throughout the Gospels (Matthew 8:20, 26:63–64; Mark 10:45), again pointing back to Daniel 7 and revealing Himself to be the divine human who ushers in and reigns over God's kingdom. Therefore, Jesus is the fulfillment of the Son of Man mentioned in Daniel 7:13–14.

> Read Matthew 26:64. What does Jesus say about the Son of Man in this verse?

Jesus's words in Matthew 24:29–31 have been interpreted in different ways. Some believe Jesus uses Daniel 7:13–14 to reference His ascension to heaven and the later destruction of Jerusalem (c. AD 70), while others believe Jesus uses Daniel 7:13–14 to describe His Second Coming. Those who hold to the first view point to the fact that in Daniel 7, the Son of Man approaches God, rather than coming from God to the earth. They also point to Matthew 26:64, where Jesus references Daniel 7 in relation to His ascension. Meanwhile, those who hold to the latter view point to several references where the Son of Man's coming seems to be a coming toward earth (Matthew 24:30, 39, 42–44). Revelation 1:7 also references Jesus's return using the language of Daniel 7.

But even though there are different interpretations of this passage, Jesus's words remind us that He is currently ruling and reigning in heaven, and He will indeed return. While the nations will tremble at His coming, His people will rejoice, knowing that their King has come to establish God's glorious kingdom on earth as it is in heaven.

> Praise Jesus for His power and glory and for making it possible to belong to a kingdom that cannot be shaken.

Live it Out

> Read Daniel 7:13–14 and Matthew 24:29–31.

Jesus is the Son of Man who has gone up in the clouds and will come again to bring God's kingdom in its fullness. As we wait for Christ's return and live in a world with nations that continue to rage, Matthew 24:29–31 and Daniel 7:13–14 give us hope as believers. These passages confirm that Jesus is, in fact, coming back, and because He is coming back, we know that we will be with our Savior one day — rescued from this current world of darkness. Such hope encourages us to look forward in anticipation as we await the day Jesus will return to bring judgment upon the wicked and justice for the oppressed, ushering all of God's people into His eternal kingdom.

Even though we wait to live in God's eternal kingdom, Matthew 24:29–31 and Daniel 7:13–14 remind us that God's kingdom is greater than any kingdom on earth. It can be easy to live in fear as wars rage and other nations threaten our own, but these Scriptures help us cling to the truth that no earthly kingdom can compare to the power of God's heavenly kingdom. Therefore, we can live in this present world and its chaotic kingdoms with peace, knowing that no matter how terrible the nations of this earth become, God's kingdom will continue to stand.

Reflect on this week's verses as you answer the following questions.

> Why is it important that Jesus is coming back?

How does knowing that God's kingdom will last forever give you peace?

How does the truth of God's eternal and unshakeable kingdom impact how you live?

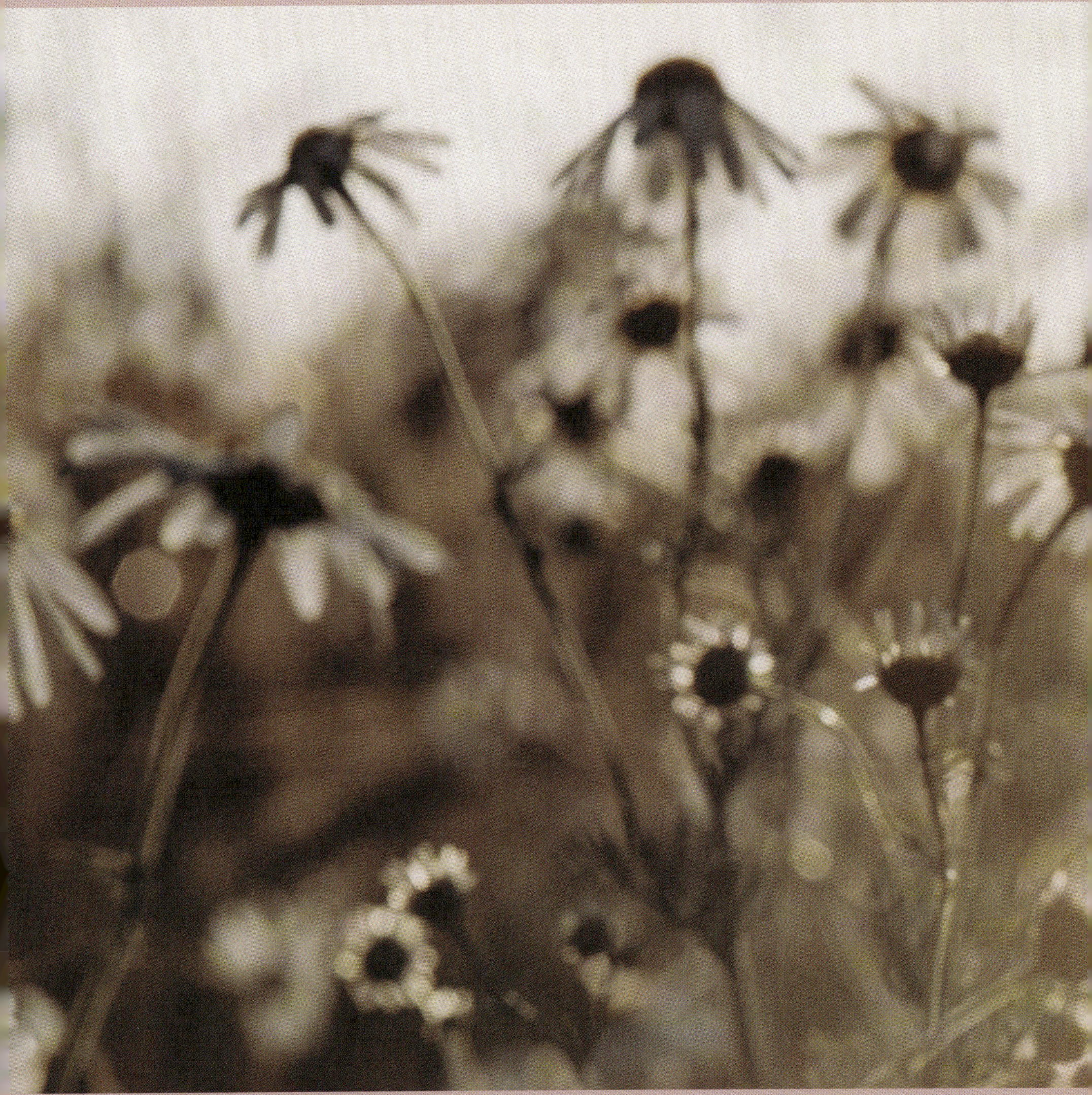

WEEK 43

Introduction

This week, as we read Hosea 1:2–3, Hosea 3:1–5, and Ephesians 5:25–32, we will see God's faithfulness to His people displayed through Christ's giving of Himself for the Church. As we trace the themes of the idolatry of God's people and Jesus's continuous faithfulness through these passages, you will be encouraged that Christ remains faithful to us even when we are unfaithful to Him.

God promises to be faithful
to His people, even when
they are unfaithful to Him.

Mark it Up: Old Testament Passage

Today, we will begin our study of Hosea 1:2–3 and 3:1–5. We will see how God promises to be faithful to His people, even when they are unfaithful to Him. Read the passage multiple times and annotate, or mark up, the text as you read. For tips and examples on annotating, see pages 188–199.

Highlight any words or phrases that point to Christ.

Make note of any attributes of God seen in the text.

Circle the words and pronouns that refer to Israel or the Israelites.

Underline any commands that God makes in these passages.

Highlight any promises that God makes in these passages.

HOSEA 1:2–3

² When the Lord first spoke to Hosea, he said this to him:

Go and marry a woman of promiscuity,

and have children of promiscuity,

for the land is committing blatant acts of promiscuity

by abandoning the Lord.

³ So he went and married Gomer daughter of Diblaim,

and she conceived and bore him a son.

HOSEA 3:1–5

¹Then the LORD said to me, "Go again; show love to a woman who is loved by another man and is an adulteress, just as the LORD loves the Israelites though they turn to other gods and love raisin cakes."

² So I bought her for fifteen shekels of silver and nine bushels of barley.

³ I said to her, "You are to live with me many days. You must not be promiscuous or belong to any man, and I will act the same way toward you."

⁴ For the Israelites must live many days without king or prince, without sacrifice or sacred pillar, and without ephod or household idols. ⁵ Afterward, the people of Israel will return and seek the LORD their God and David their king. They will come with awe to the LORD and to his goodness in the last days.

Go Deeper

> Read Hosea 1:2–3 and 3:1–5.

The book of Hosea is a book of both judgment and hope. God had long ago made a covenant with Israel, in which He promised that He would be their God and they would be His people. In other words, He would bless them, and they would worship Him alone and keep His commandments. But during the time in which Hosea is writing, the people of Israel have consistently turned from God. They have made alliances with other nations and are worshiping those nations' false gods.

> Read Hosea 1:2–3 again. What does the marriage between Hosea and Gomer represent?

Throughout the prophetic books, marriage is often used as a metaphor for God's relationship with His people (Ezekiel 16:8–21, Jeremiah 2:2, Isaiah 54:5–8), but this metaphor is the most prominent in the book of Hosea, where God calls His prophet, Hosea, to marry "a woman of promiscuity" (Hosea 1:2) as an illustration of God's uniting Himself to a sinful and fickle people who are "abandoning the Lord" (Hosea 1:2).

Given the nature of covenants in the Bible, this metaphor is entirely fitting. A covenant is a binding agreement between two parties. In fact, in a biblical sense, marriage is a form of covenant. These covenants require faithfulness—both parties are expected to uphold their end of the agreement. In a marriage, that means remaining faithful to one's spouse. For Israel, it meant remaining faithful to God and not turning from Him to worship or trust other gods. Idolatry then, is often compared to adultery, as it is in Hosea. We see that just as Israel abandoned their God, Gomer abandons Hosea to be with another man (Hosea 3:1).

> How would you expect God to react when His people abandon Him?

In these ancient covenants, when one party broke the agreement, the other was released from upholding their end of the agreement. By these human standards, God then has every right to turn from His people and allow them to be totally destroyed. But this is not His reaction. Just as Hosea knew from the outset that Gomer was promiscuous, God knew when He made His covenant with Israel that their hearts were sinful and could not be faithful (Deuteronomy 31:16–22).

However, God remains faithful to them despite their idolatry. Though He does condemn their sinfulness, disobedience, and idolatry, He does not leave them to their own destruction. He promises to remain faithful to them and to renew His covenant (Hosea 3:4–5).

> Read Hosea 14:4–7.
> Pray and thank God for His love and forgiveness toward us.

Mark it Up: New Testament Passage

Today, we will study Ephesians 5:25–32. In this passage, we will see how the relationship between Christ and the Church fulfills God's promise in Hosea to redeem His people. Read the passage multiple times and annotate, or mark up, the text as you read. For tips and examples on annotating, see page 188–199.

Highlight any words or phrases that point to Christ.

Make note of any attributes of God seen in the text.

Circle all references to the Church (including pronouns).

Underline any references to marriage that you see in the passage.

The relationship between Christ and the Church fulfills God's promise in Hosea to redeem His people.

EPHESIANS 5:25-32

25 Husbands, love your wives, just as Christ loved the church and gave himself for her 26 to make her holy, cleansing her with the washing of water by the word.

27 He did this to present the church to himself in splendor, without spot or wrinkle or anything like that, but holy and blameless. 28 In the same way, husbands are to love their wives as their own bodies. He who loves his wife loves himself. 29 For no one ever hates his own flesh but provides and cares for it, just as Christ does for the church, 30 since we are members of his body. 31 For this reason a man will leave his father and mother and be joined to his wife, and the two will become one flesh.

32 This mystery is profound, but I am talking about Christ and the church.

Make the Christ Connection

> Read Hosea 1:2–3, Hosea 3:1–5, and Ephesians 5:25–32.

In Paul's letter to the Ephesians, he is encouraging the church in their unity and identity in Christ and challenging them to walk according to the truths of the gospel. In chapter 5, Paul gives practical, day-to-day instructions for faithful Christian living, including instruction on the topic of marriage. In an aside to his instruction to husbands, we find a beautiful articulation of the Old Testament marriage metaphor brought to new light through Christ.

> In Hosea, the marriage metaphor refers to the relationship between God and Israel. What relationship is Paul referring to with his marriage metaphor in Ephesians?

In Ephesians, Paul uses marriage to speak of the faithful and sacrificial love of Christ toward the Church. Toward the end of this discourse (Ephesians 5:31), Paul quotes from Genesis 2:24, which says: "This is why a man leaves his father and mother and bonds with his wife, and they become one flesh." This is the very first mention of marriage in the Bible, and Paul uses it in his argument to make this key point: marriage, as instituted by God, has always been intended to point us toward Christ's commitment and love for His people—the Church. That is why Paul says, "This mystery is profound" (Ephesians 5:32).

More than that, however, Paul is further emphasizing that Christ is the God of the Old Testament who has come to renew His covenant with Israel. But now, the covenant is made with all people who put their faith in Him.

> How is God's covenant with His people renewed through Christ?

We saw in Hosea that God was intent on remaining faithful to His people even after they had abandoned Him. Just like Hosea would love and bring back his unfaithful wife, Gomer, God would draw His people to Himself.

But, unlike Hosea, God's plan involved more than just bringing back His unfaithful bride. It would be through Christ that His bride—the Church—would be transformed into a faithful and obedient people. Through the death and resurrection of Christ, the perfect God-man, the Church would be made clean, presented "without spot or wrinkle or anything like that, but holy and blameless" (Ephesians 5:27). We—God's people—have had all our sins washed clean and all our unfaithfulness wiped away by the blood of Christ.

Although we will still struggle with sin in this life, Christ's death has assured us that we are considered blameless now because we have been united to Him (Ephesians 5:29–31), clothed in His righteousness (Isaiah 61:10, 2 Corinthians 5:21), and sealed with the promise of redemption (Ephesians 4:30).

That redemption will come to fruition in the last days when He returns and we share in His resurrection. Then, our lives will be totally conformed to the nature and image of Christ (1 Corinthians 15:49), and we will be prepared like a bright and pure bride and will share at last in the wedding feast of our Lord (Revelation 19:7–8).

> Pray and thank God for His faithfulness in sending Christ to die for your sins and make you clean.

Live it Out

> Read Hosea 1:2–3, Hosea 3:1–5, and Ephesians 5:25–32.

This week, we have learned that by sending Christ to live and die on our behalf, God made a way for us—His unfaithful people—to be made faithful and blameless through the power of His Spirit. We will see this come to complete fruition when Jesus returns to make all things right and we, the Church, are prepared for Him like a beautiful and blameless bride.

In a different letter, Paul writes, "I am sure of this, that he who started a good work in you will carry it on to completion until the day of Christ Jesus" (Philippians 1:6). This promise is for you. Christ began His work in you when He died for your sins, and He will surely bring it to completion on the day He returns.

Reflect on this week's verses as you answer the following questions.

> How does the metaphor of marriage used for Christ and the Church impact your understanding of your relationship with God?

In what ways have you seen God remain faithful to you despite your sin?

Scripture encourages us to forgive others as Christ has forgiven us (Ephesians 4:32). How has what you have learned this week encouraged you to practice forgiveness in your life?

We strive to conform to
the Lord's identity as we learn
the depths of *hesed* love.

GOD'S *HESED* LOVE IN THE BOOK OF HOSEA

Hesed: Loving-Kindness, Faithful Love, Steadfast Love

—

(KHEH'-SED)

USED OVER 250 TIMES IN THE OLD TESTAMENT

Hosea 2:19
I will take you to be my wife forever. I will take you to be
my wife in righteousness, justice, love, and compassion.

—

The Hebrew word *hesed* does not have an exact translation into English, so our Bible translations do their best with terms like loving-kindness or steadfast love. This love is enduring and powerful, and we see it exemplified throughout the whole book of Hosea. When God's covenant people fail and rebel, God maintains His *hesed* love for them. He pursues them continuously. He is patient with them, desiring them to return to Him. When the Israelites prostitute themselves to worthless things, God maintains His *hesed* love. His loving-kindness endures, and He buys them back in accordance with their covenant.

God's love is so radical that it can be hard for us to fully understand. We do not even have an equivalent descriptor in English to convey to us the depth and breadth of *hesed* love. Nevertheless, the prophet Hosea allows us to see *hesed* love in action. Hosea is faithful to his adulterous wife in the same way that the Lord maintains His faithfulness to His people. This points us toward the *hesed* love that was displayed to us on the cross—the Son who, being completely faithful to the Father, laid down His life in place of ours. This love of the Father sent His Son to be crucified on the cross for our sins.

Though we can never measure up to that type of love, we are now compelled through Christ to live out loving-kindness and faithfulness toward one another. We seek to mimic God's steadfast love in our relationships. We strive for compassion, kindness, and grace because of the ultimate compassion, kindness, and grace that has been extended to us. Daily, we commit to loving the Lord more than we did the day before. We remain vigilant in loving Him because He first loved us. We must tend to our affection of Him, remaining faithful in our daily lives. We strive to conform to the Lord's identity as we learn the depths of *hesed* love.

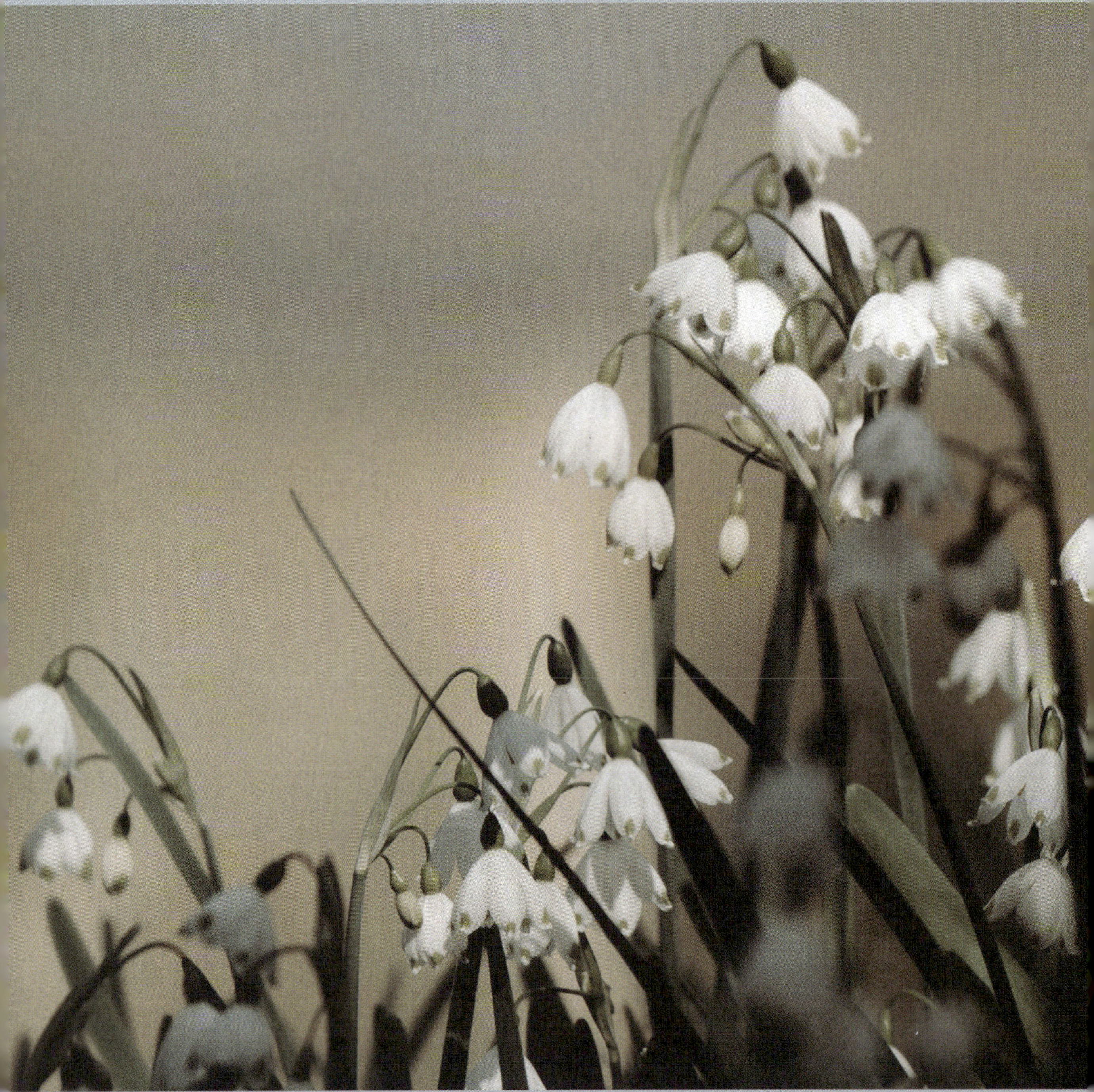

WEEK 44

Introduction

This week, we will turn our attention to the prophet Joel and his prophecy of God pouring out His Spirit on all people (Joel 2:28–29). We will see this prophecy's connection to what happens on the Day of Pentecost in Acts 2 as we look at verses 32–33, considering how, by fulfilling this prophecy, God enables us to walk in His ways.

Mark it Up: Old Testament Passage

We will begin this week by looking at the prophecy found in Joel 2:28–29 about God's Spirit. Read the passage two or three times and annotate, or mark up, the text as you read. For tips and examples on annotating, see page 188–199.

> Highlight any words or phrases that point to Christ.

> Make note of any attributes of God seen in the text.

> Underline the different groups of people mentioned in this passage.

> Circle what each of these groups will do.

> Verse 28 begins with the words, "After this . . ." What are these words referring to? What has been happening in Joel up to this point?
> (Hint: For help answering this question, read Joel 1:1–2:27.)

JOEL 2:28-29

[28] After this

I will pour out my Spirit on all humanity;

then your sons and your daughters will prophesy,

your old men will have dreams,

and your young men will see visions.

[29] I will even pour out my Spirit

on the male and female slaves in those days.

Go Deeper

> Read Joel 2:28–32.

Many of the prophetic books in the Bible begin with some kind of indication of who that prophet was, along with the time and place in which he lived. But with Joel, we get the name of his father and nothing else (Joel 1:1). Joel lived at an unspecified point in history and spoke out against the unspecified sins of God's people (most likely, those living in the southern kingdom of Judah).

Joel's message is that God will send judgment on His people because of their sins, and he frequently refers to this as "the day of the LORD" (Joel 1:15; 2:1, 11, 31; 3:14). God's people assumed this day would be a *good* thing — a day when God would come and rescue them from their enemies. Instead, Joel prophesies that it will be a day of disaster since they have turned away from Him. God's judgment will take the form of a locust swarm that will devastate their land and lead to drought (Joel 1:2–4).

> Read Jeremiah 7:3–11. As indicated in passages like this one, the people of Judah presumed that since they were God's people, they could live however they wanted to and not face judgment. How might we make similar presumptions today?

Locusts and drought were among the judgments that God told Israel they could expect in the Promised Land if they rebelled against Him (Deuteronomy 28:22, 38–42). But God also assured His people that even if judgment came, He would restore them if they repented and turned to Him with their whole heart (Deuteronomy 4:29, 30:2–3, 6).

In addition to warnings of judgment, Joel also contains calls to repentance (Joel 1:13–20, 2:12–17). God calls the people to return to Him with all their heart and Joel tells them: "Tear your hearts, not just your clothes, and return to the LORD your God" (Joel 2:12–13).

If they do this, God will bring restoration. This restoration will first involve God repaying all the abundance of which the locusts have deprived them (Joel 2:18–27). Second, it will involve God pouring out His Spirit on all people (Joel 2:28–32).

> What comfort do you think this promise of the Spirit gave to Joel's original audience?

Throughout the Old Testament, the Holy Spirit is seen working at various times. He was present at creation (Genesis 1:2) and filled certain people to fulfill tasks given to them by God (Exodus 35:30–35, Numbers 27:15–18, Judges 14:5–6). We are told that the Spirit left King Saul (1 Samuel 16:14) and that after David sinned against Bathsheba, he pleaded for God not to take His Spirit from him (Psalm 51:11). These references show us that at this point in redemptive history, God's Spirit was only given to *some* of God's people—and He could be taken away from them.

But, in Numbers 11:29, Moses expressed a longing for God to one day put His Spirit on *all* of His people. And according to Joel 2:28–32, that is exactly what God would one day do.

> In Joel 2:13, what reason does Joel give for why God's people should turn to Him? How can this encourage us to repent of our own sins today?

W44 / D3

Mark it Up: New Testament Passage

Now that we have spent time looking at Joel 2, we will turn our attention to Acts 2:32–33, which records a pivotal moment not only in the Bible but also in world history. Read the passage two or three times and annotate, or mark up, the text as you read. For tips and examples on annotating, see pages 188–199.

> Highlight any words or phrases that point to Christ.

> Make note of any attributes of God seen in the text.

> Underline any words you see echoed here from Joel 2:28–29.

> Circle God's actions in this passage, as well as Jesus's actions.

> In Acts 2:33, Peter refers to what the audience has seen and heard. What event is he referring to? (See Acts 2:1–11)

ACTS 2:32-33

[32] "God has raised this Jesus; we are all witnesses of this. [33] Therefore, since he has been exalted to the right hand of God and has received from the Father the promised Holy Spirit, he has poured out what you both see and hear."

Make the Christ Connection

> Read Joel 2:28–29 and Acts 2:32–33.

After Jesus was crucified and raised from the dead, He spent "a period of forty days" with his apostles, "speaking about the kingdom of God" (Acts 1:2–3). As that period of time drew to a close and He prepared to depart, Jesus commanded them to stay in Jerusalem and "wait for the Father's promise," referring to the arrival of the Holy Spirit who would come upon them (Acts 1:4–8).

> Read Acts 1:8 and Luke 24:46–49. What mission does Jesus give to His disciples? What is the Spirit's role in that mission?

This Spirit's arrival comes a few days later as a group of 120 of Jesus's disciples are gathered together in Jerusalem. Being the day of Pentecost, an annual religious festival prescribed in the Old Testament, Jews from all over the Roman Empire have gathered in Jerusalem. Jesus's disciples, filled with the Spirit, begin to speak to them about "the magnificent acts of God" in the languages of all the various people represented in Jerusalem that day—languages that Jesus's disciples have never learned (Acts 2:1–11)!

Naturally, some in the audience are curious about what they are witnessing. Others, taking a different approach, claim that Jesus's disciples are drunk (Acts 2:13). At this point, Peter gets up and addresses the crowd, dispelling the notion that they are drunk. (It is only nine in the morning, after all!) Rather, what the crowd is witnessing is the outpouring of God's Spirit as prophesied by Joel. Peter quotes this prophecy in its entirety to land on the critical statement that "everyone who calls on the name of the Lord will be saved" (Acts 2:21).

Peter then explains how all this is possible. He tells them that after Jesus was unjustly killed and then raised to life again, He ascended to heaven, where He "has been exalted to the right hand of God" (Acts 2:33). Being exalted, Jesus then "poured out" the Holy Spirit. Peter closes by assuring his listeners that they, too, will receive the same Spirit if they turn to Jesus (Acts 2:38–39).

> Before His crucifixion, Jesus had prepared His disciples for the coming of the Holy Spirit. Read John 15:26 and 16:7–8. According to these verses, why is Jesus's current absence a good thing?

Joel was one of many prophets who spoke of a time when God would *pour out* His Spirit (see page 86). Pentecost marked the beginning of this time, a new era in which all of God's people are indwelt—permanently—by God's Spirit. According to passages like Romans 8:9 and 1 Corinthians 12:13, part of what it means to be a Christian is to have the Spirit. Salvation includes not only the taking away of our sins but the giving of the Spirit to us (Galatians 3:10–14).

Just as God through His Spirit empowered certain people to fulfill tasks in the Old Testament, He has now empowered *all* of His people to fulfill the task of letting all nations know that "everyone who calls on the name of the Lord will be saved" (Joel 2:32).

> Spend some time in prayer, thanking God for the gift of His Spirit.

Live it Out

> Read Joel 2:28–29 and Acts 2:32–33.

Between the Gospel that bears his name and the book of Acts, no single author contributed more pages to the New Testament than Luke. Luke begins Acts by saying that in the "first narrative"—that is, in the Gospel of Luke—he wrote about "all that Jesus began to do and teach" until His ascension (Acts 1:1). The word "began" is noteworthy because it implies that Acts is a record of what Jesus—who was taken up to heaven—*continued* to do through His Spirit-empowered followers. Acts records how the good news of Jesus began to spread throughout Jerusalem, spill over into Judea and Samaria, and then take root among the nations. The book then ends with Paul preaching the gospel in the heart of the empire: Rome.

This steady progression of the gospel spreading to new frontiers is attributed to the arrival of the Holy Spirit. As Peter says in Acts 2:38–39, when we turn to Jesus in faith, we receive the Spirit. The Spirit helps us put sin to death and live holy lives (Romans 8:1–13), and He empowers us to be witnesses for Jesus. As we declare Jesus to the world around us—through the way we live and through telling others about Him—we, like the disciples in Acts, continue the work of Jesus in our own day.

Reflect on this week's verses as you answer the following questions.

> In what ways has the Spirit helped you live differently?

Spend time reading and meditating on Romans 8:14–17. What does the Spirit do according to these verses? What comfort can you take from this?

When it comes to sharing the gospel with others, what is our role? According to John 16:8, what is the Spirit's role? How might this reminder encourage you as you talk to others about Jesus?

Prophecies of the Holy Spirit

As we have learned throughout this week of our study, Joel prophesied that God would one day "pour out" the Holy Spirit on His people (Joel 2:28–29)—a prophecy that was fulfilled on the day of Pentecost (Acts 2:32–33). But Joel was not the only Old Testament prophet to look toward this day. Below, we have listed several passages from other prophets who—themselves inspired by the Holy Spirit—pointed toward this day.

> For the palace will be deserted,
> the busy city abandoned.
> The hill and the watchtower will become
> barren places forever,
> the joy of wild donkeys,
> and a pasture for flocks,
> until the Spirit from on high is poured out on us.
> Then the desert will become an orchard,
> and the orchard will seem like a forest.
>
> **ISAIAH 32:14–15**

> For I will pour water on the thirsty land
> and streams on the dry ground;
> I will pour out my Spirit on your descendants
> and my blessing on your offspring.
>
> **ISAIAH 44:3**

> "I will no longer hide my face from them, for I will pour out my Spirit on the house of Israel." This is the declaration of the Lord God.
>
> **EZEKIEL 39:29**

> After this
> I will pour out my Spirit on all humanity;
> then your sons and your daughters will prophesy,
> your old men will have dreams,
> and your young men will see visions.
> I will even pour out my Spirit
> on the male and female slaves in those days.
>
> **JOEL 2:28–29**

In Acts 2:14–21, Peter says that Joel's prophecy has been fulfilled. He goes on to say that after Jesus ascended to heaven, He then "poured out" the Spirit (Acts 2:33). Now, God's Spirit permanently indwells *all* of God's people (Romans 8:9; 1 Corinthians 12:3, 13). May we praise God for sending us the gift of the Holy Spirit—a gift that was part of His great plan of redemption all along.

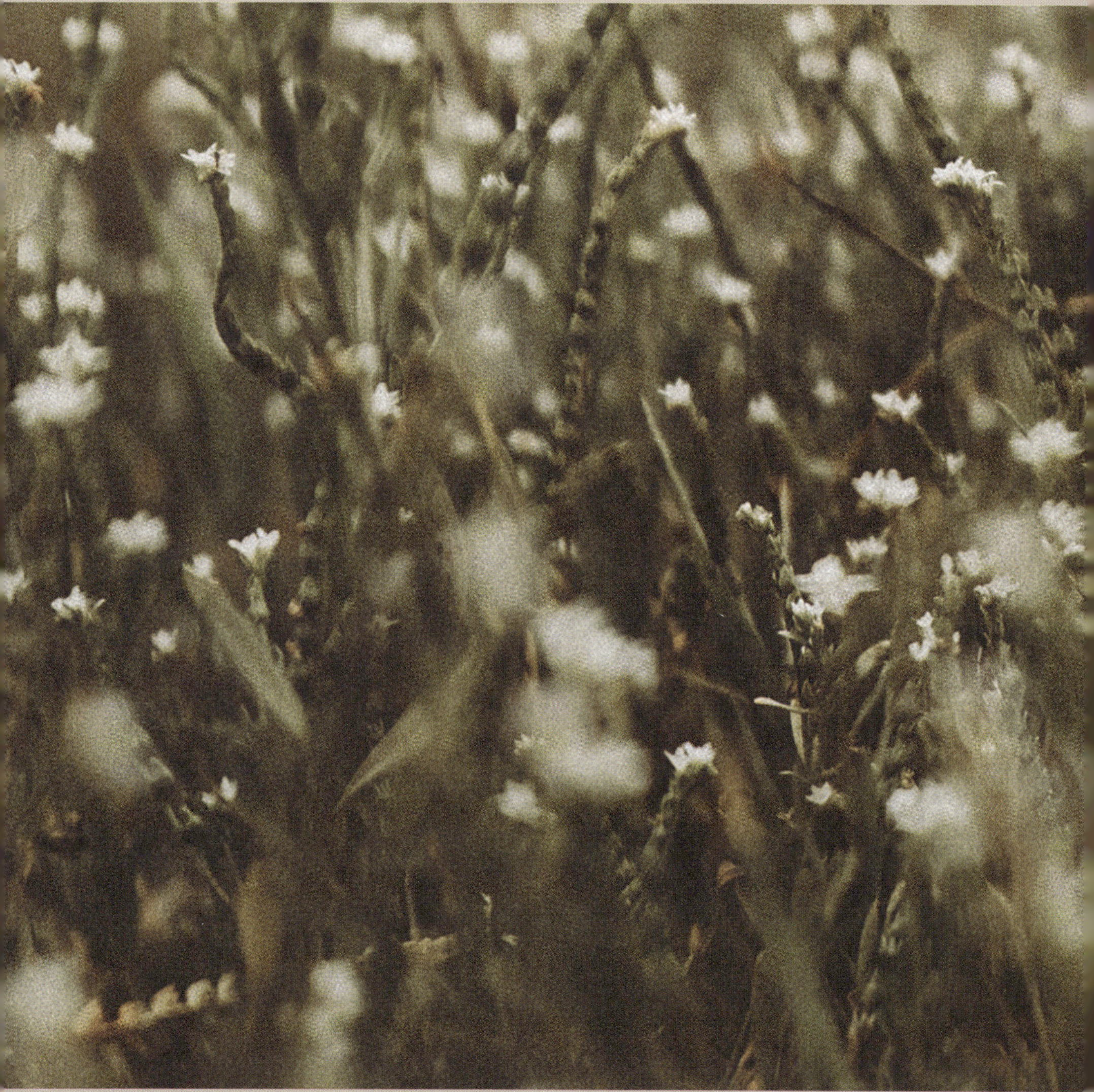

WEEK 45

Introduction

This week, we will read Amos 9:11–12 and Acts 15:15–19 as we learn about how God has brought restoration and salvation for all people through Christ. In doing so, you will be encouraged to praise God for His salvation and reflect God's heart by bringing the good news of the gospel to the nations.

W45 / D1

Mark it Up: Old Testament Passage

Today, we will begin in the Old Testament passage of Amos 9:11–12 and learn of God's promise to restore Israel and bring the nations to Himself. Read the passage two or three times and annotate, or mark up, the text as you read. For tips and examples on annotating, see pages 188–199.

Highlight any words or phrases that point to Christ.

Make note of any attributes of God seen in the text.

Circle the words "I will" where they appear in these verses.

Underline the words "so that" in verse 12. According to verse 12, what is the result of what was promised in verse 11?

According to verse 12, who will accomplish these actions?

AMOS 9:11–12

[11] In that day

I will restore the fallen shelter of David:

I will repair its gaps,

restore its ruins,

and rebuild it as in the days of old,

[12] so that they may possess

the remnant of Edom

and all the nations

that bear my name—

this is the declaration of the Lord; he will do this.

Go Deeper

> Read Amos 9:11–12.

Imagine a deteriorated building. Parts of the structure have large pieces removed. Holes litter the walls. Some windows have cracked, while others have shattered completely. Areas of the ceiling have collapsed. The building is completely useless. At this point in their history, the people of Israel can be compared to a broken building. They once stood strong because of their obedience and dedication to the Lord. But over time, they have lost their foundation. They have chosen to worship and rely on the gods of the nations rather than the one true God who truly holds them together. Now, they are broken people who are in desperate need of repair.

In the book of Amos, God uses the prophet Amos to declare words of judgment upon the Israelites. Their consistent wickedness deserves punishment, and God makes known what will happen to Israel if they do not repent (Amos 9:7–10). Yet, although God proclaims judgment upon Israel, He also promises restoration. Yes, Israel is broken and will reap the consequences of the Israelites' sin, but God promises to restore His people and repair their brokenness (Amos 9:11–15). Through this restoration, God will bring the nations to Himself, creating a people of all tribes and tongues who will praise His name.

Amos 9 continues a series of visions Amos has had about the judgment God will enact upon Israel. Such visions are hard to read, but God is just in His judgment. If we look to the earlier passages of Amos, we see how wicked Israel has become (Amos 2:4–8). God states in Amos 3:10, "The people are incapable of doing right—this is the Lord's declaration—those who store up violence and destruction in their citadels." The Israelites are wayward and disobedient, and even though God has sent previous punishments upon Israel to wake them from their disobedience, they have not listened.

> Read Amos 4:9 and 4:11. How does God describe Israel and their disobedience in these verses?

Israel has been consistently wicked, and they have refused to repent and turn back to the Lord. Therefore, there will be consequences for their disobedience. Yet God will be faithful to His people, though He will punish them. Amos 9:11–12 gives Israel hope, as God promises to restore Israel. God declares that He will "restore the fallen shelter of David" (verse 11). It is sometimes debated what precisely David's "shelter" is referring to. Most likely, though, it is a reference to David's kingly line, which—along with the kingdom of Judah and its capital city, Jerusalem—has fallen because of their waywardness. But God promises to build up His people again, restoring them so that they can be a united people who worship Him.

> Read Amos 9:13–15. How else does God promise to restore Israel, according to these verses?

This promise of restoration does not apply to the Israelites alone. Verse 12 shows how this restoration will include the nations so that the nations will bear God's name. Israel's restoration will impact the nations, bringing people from other tribes and tongues together with Israel, forming a nation of all people who worship the Lord. And it is by God's hand alone that this will be accomplished.

> Praise God for being a God of restoration and for being faithful to restore His people, even when we are unfaithful to Him.

Mark it Up: New Testament Passage

Today, we come to the New Testament passage of Acts 15:15–19 and learn how God's promise of restoration is ultimately fulfilled in Jesus, who makes a way for all people to come and know Him. Read the passage two or three times and annotate, or mark up, the text as you read. For tips and examples on annotating, see pages 188–199.

Highlight any words or phrases that point to Christ.

Make note of any attributes of God seen in the text.

Circle the verbs (or the action words) in verse 16. What does God promise to do?

Underline the words "so that" in verse 17.
What will be the result of the restoration, according to verse 17?

Draw a box around the word "therefore" in verse 19. According to this verse, what should not be done in light of what is proclaimed in verses 16–19?

ACTS 15:15–19

¹⁵ And the words of the prophets agree with this, as it is written:

¹⁶ After these things I will return

and rebuild David's fallen tent.

I will rebuild its ruins

and set it up again,

¹⁷ so that the rest of humanity may seek the Lord—

even all the Gentiles

who are called by my name—

declares the Lord who makes these things ¹⁸ known from long ago.

¹⁹ Therefore, in my judgment, we should not cause difficulties

for those among the Gentiles who turn to God.

Make the Christ Connection

> Read Amos 9:11–12 and Acts 15:15–19.

The Israelites were God's chosen people, yet God's plan of redemption is not exclusive to Israel alone. God desires all nations to come to know Him, and we see this truth come to fruition as we continue in our journey through the Bible. In Acts 15:15–19, we learn how the Old Testament points to God's desire and promise to bring salvation to the nations.

Acts 15:15–19 takes place during the Jerusalem Council. At this time in the early church, the apostles and elders have gathered to discuss the Gentiles' inclusion in God's family. This council takes place because some were teaching that circumcision and obedience to the Law were necessary in order for Gentiles to become followers of Christ (Acts 15:1–5). Peter responds to this issue by declaring that God's plan of salvation includes both Jews and Gentiles and that salvation comes through grace alone (Acts 15:7–11). James stands up to affirm Peter's words, and he uses Amos 9:11–12 to do so, explaining how the Gentiles are able to seek the Lord because of God's restoration.

> Go back a few chapters and read Acts 13:46–48. What do these verses teach? What was the Gentiles' response to this message?

What is discussed in Acts 15 connects to Amos 9:11–12 as it shows God's desire for the Gentiles to receive salvation, too. Ultimately, the Gentiles are able to receive this salvation through Christ. While Amos 9:11–12 was partially fulfilled when God's people were restored from the Exile, Jesus ultimately made restoration possible through His death and resurrection, which we read about in the New Testament.

Christ's sacrifice restores us in our relationship with God and transforms us into a people who joyfully serve and honor the Lord. It is because of His sacrifice that both Jews and Gentiles can belong to God's family. Jesus invites Gentiles to come and know Him, and His work on the cross has removed the wall of hostility that once divided Jews and Gentiles (Ephesians 2:11–15).

> Why is it important that God has made salvation available to all people?

The restoration promised in Amos 9:11–12 is greater than the Israelites could have ever imagined. God's plan of salvation was not for one group alone but for all nations, making it possible for anyone to receive forgiveness and be called a child of God. Because of God's fulfilled plan of redemption and restoration through Christ, people from all tribes and tongues are able to come together and worship the Lord, spreading His name and glory all over the world.

> Spend some time in prayer, thanking God for the salvation and restoration that He has made available for all people.

Live it Out

Read Amos 9:11–12 and Acts 15:15–19.

God is a God of restoration, and because of His work through Christ, He brings about restoration and salvation for all people who put their trust in Him. The restoration that God promises in Amos 9:11–12—and that Jesus ultimately fulfills—moves us to respond in gratitude to the Lord. We rejoice that God is a God who makes salvation possible for all people. He does not limit His grace to one group of people. He is not partial to some people, inviting them to know Him while shutting the door of salvation in the faces of others. God's heart is for all people to come to know Him and call Him Lord and Father (1 Timothy 2:3–4). Such a wondrous truth should cause us to lift our voices in praise to our God whose invitation of salvation is open to all.

As believers, God's heart for the nations, as well as the message of the gospel, encourages us to care about the nations. Rather than sharing the gospel with only those who are like us, the gospel motivates us to move toward those of different nationalities and backgrounds. The Great Commission calls us, as believers, to make disciples of all nations (Matthew 28:19), and we should take this call seriously. This could look like sharing the gospel with those in our neighborhoods or perhaps traveling to different countries to preach the gospel. God's heart for the nations should be our heart as well, so let us respond to God's great salvation by ensuring that all people hear God's invitation to come and know Him.

Reflect on this week's verses as you answer the following questions.

> How has this week's study caused you to consider the importance of the nations?

Why is it important to share the gospel with all nations?

What are some practical ways you can reflect God's heart for the nations?

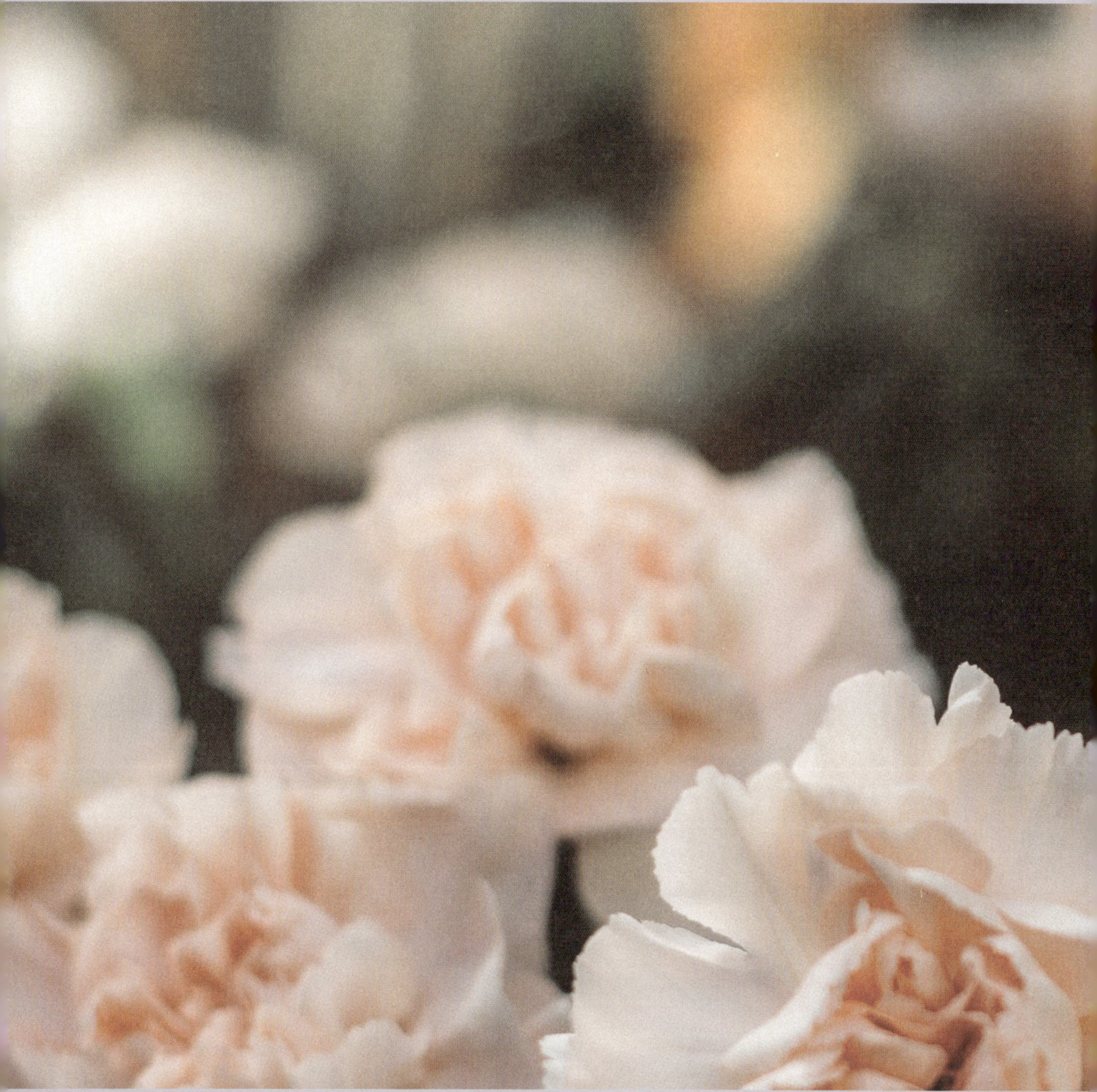

WEEK 46

Introduction

This week, we will learn that Jesus is the true and better Jonah by tracing Jonah's time in the belly of the fish and Jesus's time in the grave through Jonah 1:17 and Matthew 12:40. In response, you will be encouraged to thank God for His sacrificial obedience that brought us life through repentance, and you will be challenged to be like Jesus by faithfully and obediently sharing the gospel with those around you.

Mark it Up: Old Testament Passage

This week, we will study Jonah 1:17 and explore the ways in which Jonah was a forerunner of Jesus. Read the passage two or three times and annotate, or mark up, the text as you read. For tips and examples on annotating, see pages 188–199.

> Highlight any words or phrases that point to Christ.

> Make note of any attributes of God seen in the text.

> Circle the word "appointed." What does this word tell us about God's power?

> How many days and nights was Jonah in the belly of the fish? Why might this number be significant?

JONAH 1:17

¹⁷ The Lord appointed a great fish to swallow Jonah,

and Jonah was in the belly of the fish three days and three nights.

Go Deeper

> Read Jonah 1.

Jonah is another prophet in a long line of prophets sent to deliver warnings to wicked and rebellious people. God sends Jonah to prophesy to the Ninevites—a particularly violent group and enemies of the Israelite people. However, Jonah decides not to obey God's instruction and instead takes matters into his own hands (Jonah 1:3). Jonah does not want them to have the opportunity to repent; he does not want God to extend mercy to them (Jonah 4:1–2).

> Why might Jonah want God to withhold mercy from the Ninevites?

Instead of going toward Nineveh, Jonah flees to the farthest place He can go from where God called him to go. In an effort to flee God's presence, Jonah boards a ship to Tarshish. While aboard the boat, the Lord sends a storm that troubles the other passengers, and they become afraid. After Jonah informs the ship's crew that the storm is a result of his disobedience, Jonah tells the men to throw him into the water so that the storm will cease.

The men in the boat are not familiar with Jonah's God, yet they display more fear and faith in the God of creation than Jonah does. The men cry out to God for mercy as they fear that throwing Jonah overboard might invite God's wrath upon them. However, to save their lives, they agree to throw Jonah into the sea. This is also Jonah's attempt to escape God's command once and for all as Jonah tries to end his own life. Yet the God who made the sea and dry land (Jonah 1:9) displays His sovereignty by appointing a large fish to swallow Jonah. But this is not Jonah's end, for the fish eventually spits him onto dry land, saving his life and giving Jonah another chance to obey.

> Read Psalm 139:7–8. What has Jonah failed to remember about who God is? How do Jonah's actions contradict what he says he believes about God in Jonah 1:9?

Jonah's story proves that there is nowhere anyone can run from the presence of God. The God who created all things is sovereign over all things, exercising control over even the chaotic waters of the sea. When sinful men disobey God, He gives mercy unmerited, extending that mercy even to those who seek to hide from His presence.

As we look at Jonah's life, we cannot help but see his great failures as a prophet. Yet still, Jonah's story points forward to a greater prophet—One who was radically obedient, even to death on a cross. The true and better Prophet, Jesus, would also offer up His own life—but not to evade obedience. Instead, Jesus would willingly and humbly submit Himself to death in order to bring life to all those who would believe in Him.

> Have you ever been afraid to obey God or even refused one of His commands? How have you responded in the past to the commands of God that you find difficult? Pray a prayer of gratitude for God's mercy to you even in your disobedience.

Mark it Up: New Testament Passage

Today, we will see how Jesus is the true and better Jonah. Read Matthew 12:40 two or three times and annotate, or mark up, the text as you read. For tips and examples on annotating, see pages 188–199.

Highlight any words or phrases that point to Christ.

Make note of any attributes of God seen in the text.

Who is speaking in this passage? Who are they speaking to?

Circle the phrase "three days and three nights." We also saw this phrase appear in Jonah 1:17. Why might this phrase be repeated in Matthew 12:40?

What do you think Jesus is referring to when He mentions being "in the heart of the earth"?

What are some similarities between "the belly of the fish" and "the heart of the earth"?

MATTHEW 12:40

⁴⁰ For as Jonah was in the belly of the huge fish three days and three nights,

so the Son of Man will be in the heart of the earth three days and three nights.

Make the Christ Connection

Read Jonah 1:17 and Matthew 12:38–41.

In Matthew 12:38, a group of Pharisees approach Jesus and ask Him for a sign. They are once again trying to test Jesus and His claim to be the Messiah. Jesus notes that their demand for a sign is a mark of wickedness. They do not truly want to know who Jesus really is, but rather, they want to prove that Jesus is a blasphemer. As such, Jesus refuses to give them a sign at that moment but tells them that they will see the sign of the prophet Jonah. Jesus then explains that just as Jonah went into the belly of the fish for three days and three nights, so Jesus will go into the heart of the earth for three days and three nights. In saying this, Jesus alludes to His own death and burial to come.

In what ways does Christ's death mirror the narrative of Jonah in Jonah 1?

Though Christ's death will be reminiscent of Jonah's time in the belly of the fish, the circumstances of Jesus's time in the grave will not be a result of disobedience. Jonah attempted to flee from God and avoid bringing God's word of repentance to the Ninevites, but Jesus came to earth precisely for the purpose of calling sinners to repentance (Luke 5:31–32). Not only did Jesus bring the message of the gospel to the wicked and sinful, but Jesus was the Word of God who made His dwelling among them (John 1:14).

> Reread Jonah 1 and then read Philippians 2:5–8. In what ways was Jonah disobedient to God? In what ways was Jesus obedient to God?

> Next, read Jonah 3:10–4:2. How does Jonah's response to God's mercy to the Ninevites differ from the heart and life of Jesus?

While Jonah sought death in order to escape obedience to God, Jesus submitted to death in perfect obedience to God's will. No one took Jesus's life, but Jesus allowed Himself to be tortured and killed so that God's mercy might reach the whole world. Jonah desired God to withhold His mercy from the wicked Ninevites, but Jesus obediently died for His enemies while they were still sinners.

The repentance of the Ninevites was only a precursor to all who would one day repent and believe in Jesus. Though Jonah rebelled against God, Jonah's deliverance from the fish's mouth led to the Ninevites' salvation. Yet Christ would rise from the grave and bring salvation to all those who would repent and trust in Him.

> Write a prayer of gratitude for Jesus's obedience that brought salvation to all who believe.

Live it Out

> Read Jonah 1:17 and Matthew 12:40.

God's mercy to us in Christ has the power to change our lives. Those who believe in Jesus are spared from the coming destruction, just as the Ninevites were saved from God's wrath. Jesus is the true and better Prophet—One who submitted completely to God's instruction. Because Jesus was obedient to God, we have the opportunity to repent.

Jesus willingly went to the grave, facing a very real but temporary death so that we would not have to face death eternally. Jesus died for us and instead of us. He bore the punishment of our sin so that we would not have to bear it ourselves. Unlike Jonah, Jesus was selfless. He gave His very life so that we could have life eternally. This is the ultimate act of God's mercy.

The gospel requires that we set aside our disdain for others and care about their need for Jesus. God calls us to make disciples. We have the choice to respond like Jonah or like Jesus. Just as Christ did not allow our wickedness to continue to separate us from God, we cannot withhold the good news from others just because they are different from us or have offended us.

Reflect on this week's verses as you answer the following questions.

> Who are you holding contempt for in your heart? Are you withholding the truth of God's mercy from them? Ask God to search your heart and reveal any ways in which you may want God to withhold His mercy from others.

How might God be calling you to obedience in this season of your life?

How does God's mercy change our lives and the way we interact with others?

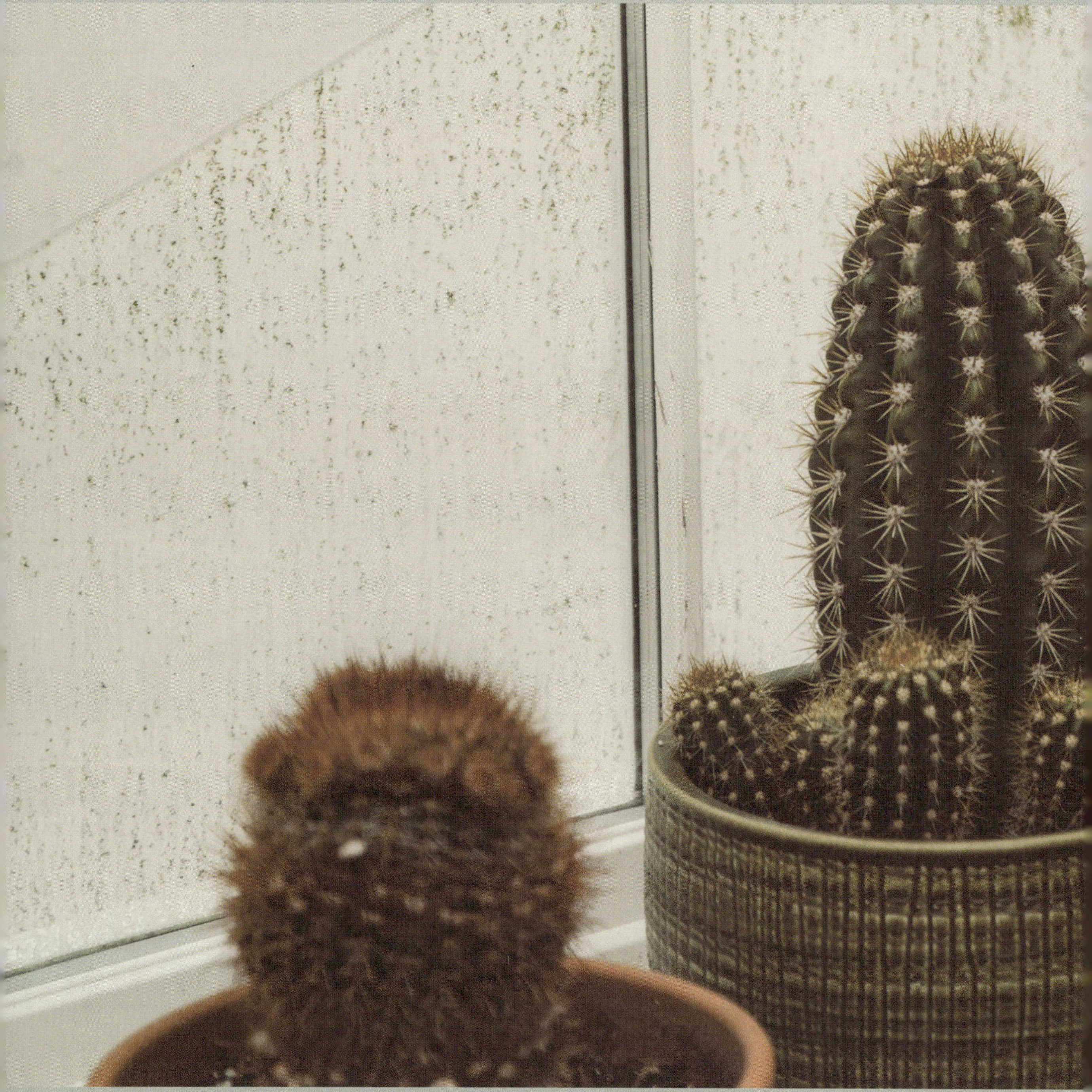

WEEK 47

Introduction

This week, we will read Micah 5:2 and Matthew 2:4–6. In looking at these passages, we will not only see how Christ is the promised Messiah from the line of David, but we will also see how Christ's fulfillment of this role and prophecy can give us hope for the future, pointing our attention beyond our current circumstances.

Mark it Up: Old Testament Passage

Today, we will study Micah 5:2 and begin to see how the promised ruler in this passage refers to Christ. Read the passage multiple times and annotate, or mark up, the text as you read. For tips and examples on annotating, see pages 188–199.

> Highlight any words or phrases that point to Christ.

> Make note of any attributes of God seen in the text.

> Circle references to Israel or cities within Israel.

> Underline words or phrases that refer to the "ruler" in this passage.

> Read the next four verses (Micah 5:3–6). Make note of the things this ruler does for the people of Israel.

MICAH 5:2

² Bethlehem Ephrathah,

you are small among the clans of Judah;

one will come from you

to be ruler over Israel for me.

His origin is from antiquity,

from ancient times.

Go Deeper

Read Micah 5:2–6.

Like most of the prophetic books in the Bible, the book of Micah contains a mixed message of both judgment and hope. The people of Israel continuously turn from their covenant with God, and God continuously uses prophets like Micah to deliver His Word to the people. Through Micah's words, the Lord tells the people of His judgment on their unfaithfulness as well as His steadfast love for them.

Read Micah 1:2–7. Who is receiving God's judgment and why?

Micah opens with this grim description of God's judgment, in which mountains will melt and valleys will split apart (Micah 1:4). The earth and all that is in it will be judged, and Micah quickly tells us why: "All this will happen because of Jacob's rebellion and the sins of the house of Israel" (Micah 1:5).

The first three chapters of this book further outline the details of both God's judgment and the people's sin. God's people have turned from His covenant, His commands, and His instructions.

Read Micah 4:1–2, 5–7. What does God promise to do in the last days?

In chapter 4, Micah shifts from a message of judgment to a message of hope. Here, he tells of God's promise to bring redemption and restoration in the last days. He will establish His house on top of the mountains. This is a total restoration—God's judgment on the people in Micah 1:4 was that the mountains would be destroyed, but here they are restored and the place of His home. The idolatrous people will worship God alone forever and ever (Micah 4:5). Those who experienced God's judgment will be restored (Micah 4:6). And He—the Lord—will reign forever and ever (Micah 4:7).

> Read 1 Samuel 16:1, 13. What is the significance of Bethlehem?

While Bethlehem was a small town, it was not by any means insignificant to Israel. Their greatest king—King David—had been a shepherd in Bethlehem before his anointing. It was His hometown, and though David later lived and reigned in Jerusalem, in Micah 5:2, Micah alerts the people that the promised Messiah, the Son of David (2 Samuel 7:12–13), would also come from Bethlehem. It is this King that the people should look for. It is this King who will bring the Lord's restoration and shepherd His people to the ends of the earth (Micah 5:4).

Mark it Up: New Testament Passage

Today, we will read Matthew 2:4–6 and see how Jesus's birth in Bethlehem fulfilled the prophecy of Micah. Read the passage multiple times and annotate, or mark up, the text as you read. For tips and examples on annotating, see pages 188–199.

> Highlight any words or phrases that point to Christ.

> Make note of any attributes of God seen in the text.

> Circle any references to Bethlehem.

> Look back at the original passage in Micah (Micah 5:2). Underline places where the prophecy in Matthew differs from where the same prophecy is given in Micah.

MATTHEW 2:4-6

⁴ So he assembled all the chief priests and scribes of the people

and asked them where the Messiah would be born.

⁵ "In Bethlehem of Judea," they told him,

"because this is what was written by the prophet:

⁶ And you, Bethlehem, in the land of Judah,

are by no means least among the rulers of Judah:

Because out of you will come a ruler

who will shepherd my people Israel."

Make the Christ Connection

> Read Micah 5:2–4 and Matthew 2:4–6.

The context of Matthew 2 is a well-known part of the Christmas story — the story of the wise men who follow a star to Bethlehem. These wise men were scholars and students of the stars. And since astronomical events like this star were often believed to be connected to the birth of kings, they left their homeland in search of this newly born King. It is possible that they were even familiar with the Hebrew Scriptures. If so, they may have had the words of Numbers 24:17 in mind: "A star will come from Jacob, and a scepter will arise from Israel."

> Read Matthew 2:1–2. Why do you think the wise men went to Jerusalem?

_____

_____

_____

_____

_____

_____

_____

When these wise men from the east saw the star that signified the birth of a Jewish King, they naturally went to Jerusalem in search of Him, as Jerusalem was known as the Holy City where the kings of Israel have always ruled.

At this time, there is a different king of the Jews on the throne — King Herod — the man the Roman Empire placed in charge of Judea to appease the Jewish people. Herod is prone to violence and fearful of anyone who threatens his rule, so when he hears these wealthy wise men speak of a new king, he is not happy (Matthew 2:3). He assembles all the Jewish religious leaders and scholars and asks them about the birth of this King.

These leaders and scholars immediately direct the wise men — and Herod — to Bethlehem, for Micah had prophesied that the Messiah would come from that small town (Micah 5:2).

> In your annotations, we asked you to compare Matthew's quote of Micah 5:2 with the actual passage. Look at the differences you noticed. Why do you think Matthew makes the changes he does?

The slight differences in wording between Micah 5:2 and Matthew 2:6 should not alarm us — in fact, Matthew likely made these adjustments only to emphasize and consolidate certain aspects of the passage from Micah. Referring to Bethlehem as being "in the land of Judah" emphasized that the One who was born would be from Israel's royal tribe, Judah. Changing the wording from "small" to "by no means least" emphasizes that although Bethlehem was once small, it had gained great significance by being the birthplace of the Messiah, the Son of God. The final addition of the words "who will shepherd my people Israel" is merely a way to incorporate a line that appears later in the Micah passage (Micah 5:4).

> How does Jesus fulfill the prophecy of Micah?

Jesus — the promised Messiah — was indeed born in Bethlehem as Micah had prophesied (Luke 2:4). He is from the line of David (Matthew 1:1) and the tribe of Judah. Later on in His earthly ministry, Jesus refers to Himself as "the Good Shepherd" (John 10:11), not just of Israel but of the whole world. He came first to inaugurate His rule through His death and resurrection, but He will return to fully establish His kingdom and rule over the whole earth (Revelation 22:3).

Live it Out

> Read Micah 5:2–4 and Matthew 2:4–6.

This week's reading focused on the prophecy of Micah, which predicted that the birth of the Messiah would take place in Bethlehem. Our reading in Matthew revealed that Christ did indeed fulfill this prophecy when He was born. He is indeed the promised King from the Old Testament. Knowing that He has come already to inaugurate His kingdom gives us confidence and hope that He is indeed coming again to fully establish His kingdom.

Reflect on this week's verses as you answer the following questions.

> Micah's prophecy brought hope in the midst of Israel's despair. How does the truth of Jesus's birth, death, and resurrection bring hope to any despair you may be facing?

In what areas of your life are you awaiting restoration?

Pray and ask God to give you hope and to help you trust Him as you await that restoration.

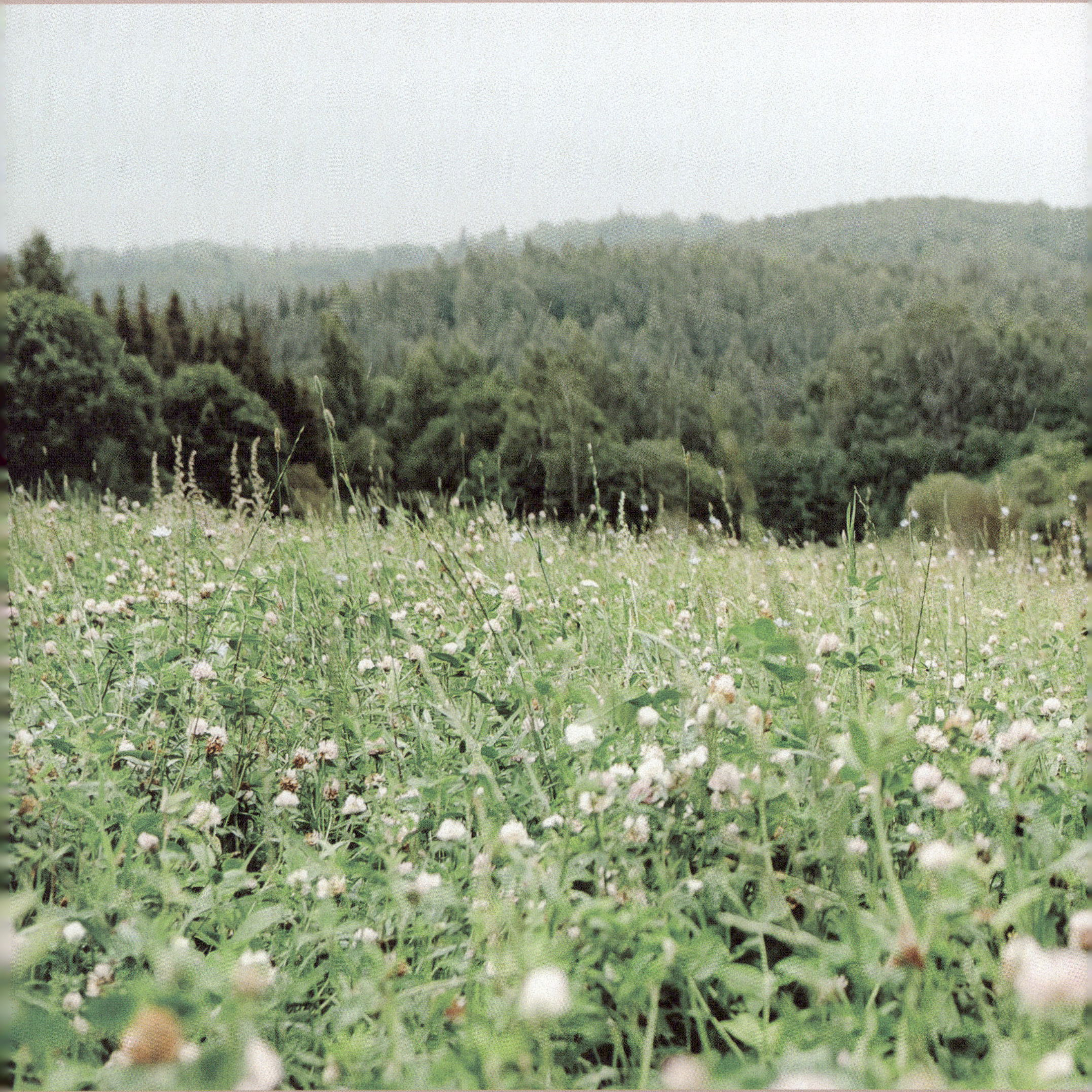

WEEK 48

Introduction

This week, we will study Habakkuk 2:4 and Romans 1:16–17 and learn that we, as believers, receive Christ's righteousness by faith. As we do so, we will be encouraged by the truth that those in Christ persevere through trials in confidence of God's promise of salvation to all who believe.

Mark it Up: Old Testament Passage

Today, we will study Habakkuk 2:4, where we will see God's response to Habakkuk's confusion about the coming Babylonian invasion. We will learn that God will not tolerate wickedness forever and calls His people to press forward in faith with confidence in Him. Read Habakkuk 2:4 multiple times and annotate, or mark up, the text as you read. For tips and examples on annotating, see pages 188–199.

Highlight any words or phrases that point to Christ.

Make note of any attributes of God seen in the text.

Who is speaking in this passage?

Draw a circle around the word "his" — a reference to the Chaldeans or Babylonians (see Habakkuk 1:5–11). How is he described in this verse?

Draw a box around the description of the "righteous one."

HABAKKUK 2:4

⁴ Look, his ego is inflated;

he is without integrity.

But the righteous one will live by his faith.

Go Deeper

> Read Habakkuk 2:4.

When you hear the words "righteous" and "faith" together in one verse, you may expect such a verse to be found in the New Testament. You might immediately think of your salvation—remembering that you are saved by faith in Jesus Christ and made righteous before God. This is true! But what do righteousness and faith mean in the context of the Old Testament prophetic book of Habakkuk?

> Read Habakkuk 1:1–11. This passage can be divided into two parts. What are the two parts? (Hint: Who is speaking in each part?)

The book of Habakkuk jumps right into a complaint from Habakkuk in which he struggles to reconcile God's character with the corruption he witnesses in Judah and the surrounding nations. Habakkuk asks God a big question that may sound familiar: "How long, Lord, must I call for help and you do not listen . . . ?" (Habakkuk 1:2a). As we witness injustice and chaos in our world, it can be easy to feel that God is turning a blind eye. But God hears Habakkuk's cry and answers him.

What a beautiful truth to remember—God does listen to us! And in God's reply to Habakkuk, He clues the prophet in on His plan. But God's answer is not what Habakkuk might expect. God tells him that the Chaldeans, or Babylonians, will be the tool of punishment on Judah for their sins (Habakkuk 2:6). God will judge Judah's evil by inflicting more evil upon them. The Babylonians will trample Judah's cities and bring their people into captivity.

> Read Habakkuk 1:12–2:1. What is Habakkuk's question to God in these verses? (Hint: look at verse 13.)

Habakkuk now has a problem. He knows that God is pure, unable to look upon wrongdoing (verse 13). And yet, God is allowing evil to overcome evil. God seems to be tolerating those who are treacherous. *What does this say about God?* And yet, even in the midst of these big faith questions, Habakkuk clings to what He knows to be true of God: God is eternal, holy, a judge, and Habakkuk's rock. Habakkuk 2:1 describes Habakkuk patiently waiting for the Lord to answer him again—to help Habakkuk wrestle with this news and what He knows of God's character.

And God answers once again.

> Read Habakkuk 2:2–20. How many times does the Lord pronounce woe on Babylon in these verses? What does this teach us about God's justice?

Habakkuk is right. God will not turn a blind eye to the violence of the Babylonians. God pronounces five woe oracles that will come upon this evil nation. God will vindicate His people and judge their captors.

In Habakkuk 2:2, God instructs Habakkuk to write down this vision and write it clearly on tablets so that it may be easily accessible to the people. Though judgment is coming, God will come out to save His people—to save His anointed (Habakkuk 3:13). And what is His instruction in the meantime? God tells Habakkuk that the righteous one will live by his faith (Habakkuk 2:4).

> Reread Habakkuk 2:4. Why can the righteous have faith in God?

God encourages His people to live by faith, to persevere through Babylon's wickedness, and to have faith that God's purposes will come about. God will not turn a blind eye to suffering. God will not forsake His covenants. God will not forsake His people.

Mark it Up: New Testament Passage

Indeed, God did not turn a blind eye to His people's suffering but sent His only Son to suffer in their place—to pay the cost of sin so that His people could remain in relationship with Him forever. Today, you will study Romans 1:16–17 and see how this relationship is possible. Read this passage multiple times and annotate, or mark up, the text as you read. For tips and examples on annotating, see pages 188–199.

Highlight any words or phrases that point to Christ.

Make note of any attributes of God seen in the text.

Highlight the word "gospel." What is the gospel? Try writing a definition in your own words in the margin.

Now, circle the conjunction "because" and underline everything after that word in verse 16. How does this clause help us understand why Paul, the author, is not ashamed?

Finally, draw a box around the word "it" wherever you see it in these verses. What do you think "it" is referring to, and how does defining this word in each instance help you understand this passage?

ROMANS 1:16–17

¹⁶ For I am not ashamed of the gospel, because it is the power of God for salvation

to everyone who believes, first to the Jew, and also to the Greek.

¹⁷ For in it the righteousness of God is revealed from faith to faith,

just as it is written: The righteous will live by faith.

Make the Christ Connection

Read Habakkuk 2:4 and Romans 1:16–17.

How can we cling to hope amid trials? Live by faith. This was God's encouragement to the people of Judah through the prophet Habakkuk upon news of their looming captivity. Yes, Judah experienced judgment for the people's sin, but God promised that He would not tolerate Babylonian treachery forever (Habakkuk 1:13, 2:16). The righteous will live by faith—faith that God is who He says He is. As God encouraged Habakkuk to persevere in faith, so too believers today are made righteous by their faith in Christ.

The heartbeat of Romans 1:16–17 is the gospel—the ultimate proof that God is with and for His people. God sent His perfect Son, Jesus, from heaven to take on the punishment of sin that we deserve. Because Jesus provided salvation from sin, God's people are free to walk with Him—to live in His presence, love, and mercy. They are counted righteous as His Son is righteous.

Read Galatians 3:11. Where does righteousness *not* come from?

_____

_____

_____

In a letter to the Galatians, the Apostle Paul quotes Habakkuk 2:4 to remind believers that the Law failed to produce righteousness and instead further condemned God's people—for they were unable to love God with their hearts and their actions. Without Christ, humanity is corrupt in sin.

The Israelites could have never earned their way to God. Instead, it was by faith in Him—even in a seemingly hopeless situation—that they would experience God's deliverance. This was a faith that one day, God would right the wrongs and save His people through a Messiah. Jesus is this Messiah.

Read Romans 3:22–24. How does a person receive Christ's righteousness?

_____

_____

A person receives the righteousness of God by grace through faith in Jesus. It is only through believing in Christ that righteousness comes—it is not by performance, lineage, or merit. Paul, the author of Romans, reminds his readers that every person has fallen short of the glory of God—no one can earn God's favor in their own strength. At the time when Paul pens this letter, the Roman church needs this reminder.

As the most powerful city in the world at this point in history, Rome likely feels like an untamable beast, much like Babylon in Habakkuk's time. To make matters worse, the Jewish and Gentile believers in Rome are butting heads within the church. The Jewish believers had been expelled from Rome under the reign of the Emperor Claudius in c. AD 49. Now, upon their return after Claudius's death, the Jewish and Gentile Christians need to reintegrate and reconcile with one another.

Paul reminds the Roman church that sin humbles both the Jew and the Gentile—for everyone needs to be saved by grace through faith in Jesus. Jewish believers are no better than their Gentile brothers and sisters, whom Paul refers to as "the Greek" in Romans 1:17. Their righteousness is not found in obeying the Law but in believing in God's Son for salvation.

> Read Romans 1:16–17. Why is Paul so emphatically unashamed of the gospel?

By referencing Habakkuk, Paul is turning the attention of the Roman church to a time when God called His people to be faithful even amidst coming hardship. Now, God has proven Himself faithful by sending Christ to live and die so that His people may be saved. How much more can they have faith now? They do not need to be ashamed or afraid, for the gospel is their power and their righteousness. All they must do is believe.

Live it Out

> Read Habakkuk 2:4 and Romans 1:16–17.

This week, we met a prophet who kept faith in God's character, even amid the horrific news of a coming invasion. We also met the Roman church, which experienced division between Jewish and Gentile believers within the world's most important city—Rome. Their presence there was vital to spread the gospel throughout Europe. How did Paul encourage them?

Paul reminds the Roman church of the truth of the gospel that unites them: they are all sinners made righteous by the power of God (Romans 1:16). Though they face big battles, this truth ties them together. They will persevere through trials by keeping this faith—keeping their eyes fixed on God and His great love for them, proven in the person and work of Jesus.

What does this mean for us today? Life is full of curveballs—surprises that often make little sense to our finite minds. Like Habakkuk, we may feel confused at what our circumstances communicate about God's character. Like the Roman church, we may be faced with challenges amid an already overwhelming gospel call. But these passages teach us that we can persevere in faith and rejoice in God's sovereignty, no matter the outcome, just as Habakkuk learned (Habakkuk 3:17–19).

Faith changes everything, for by faith, we receive Christ. Even in the harshest diagnosis or the fiercest betrayal, we can keep our eyes fixed on Jesus, for He is always our solid ground. May we never be ashamed of the gospel.

Reflect on this week's verses as you answer the following questions.

> How are you tempted to earn favor with God? How does it encourage you that you are already righteous if you profess faith in Christ?

Have your circumstances ever made you doubt God's goodness? If so, how did you wrestle with this? How did you persevere?

Have you ever found yourself ashamed of the gospel or afraid to share the good news? How does focusing on Romans 1:16–17 encourage you to overcome these feelings?

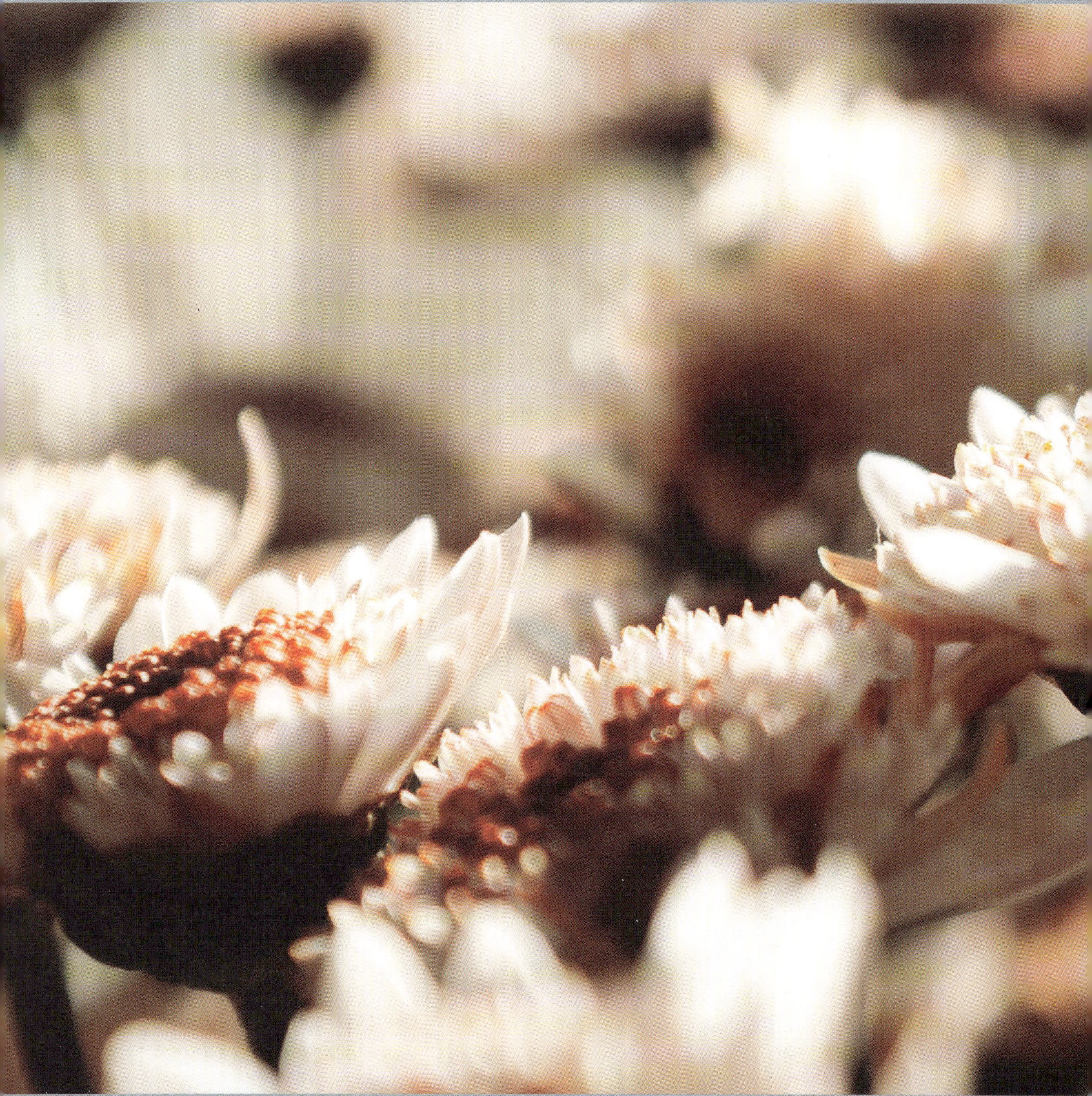

WEEK 49

Introduction

This week, we will learn that Jesus is the long-promised, humble King of Israel as we trace the theme of the King who rides on a donkey through the passages of Zechariah 9:9 and John 12:12–16. In response, we will be encouraged to adore Jesus for His humility that brought us salvation, and we will be challenged to emulate Christ's humility.

Mark it Up: Old Testament Passage

Today, we will study Zechariah 9:9, a prophecy that ultimately points toward Jesus. Read the passage two or three times and annotate, or mark up, the text as you read. For tips and examples on annotating, see pages 188–199.

Highlight any words or phrases that point to Christ.

Make note of any attributes of God seen in the text.

Circle any words that describe the King that Zechariah prophesies about. What kind of King is being depicted?

Why might a King who rides on a donkey be described as humble?

ZECHARIAH 9:9

⁹ Rejoice greatly, Daughter Zion!

Shout in triumph, Daughter Jerusalem!

Look, your King is coming to you;

he is righteous and victorious,

humble and riding on a donkey,

on a colt, the foal of a donkey.

Go Deeper

> Read Zechariah 9:9–12.

How would you expect an important person to arrive in town? A government official or king would probably ride in a fancy car surrounded by security guards. But the prophet Zechariah tells us about a King whose entry was a lot less glamorous.

Zechariah, a prophet after the exilic period, was appointed by God to prophesy to the remnant of God's people who had come back from the Exile (Zechariah 1:3–4). While he warns them about the dangers of doing the exact same things that caused their suffering, Zechariah also gives them a message of hope and expectation. Zechariah tells them of a Messiah and King who will come to redeem them from their sin and deliver them from their own hearts of wickedness (Zechariah 9:9). However, this King will be different from what the people expect.

In Zechariah's day, it was common for kings to ride in on a mule. Mules are very similar in stature to horses, and they signified dignity and power during this time. But the King whom Zechariah describes rides on a donkey—a smaller and much less impressive animal. The promised Messiah and King will display his humility by choosing not to align himself with symbols of power.

> How is the King whom Zechariah describes different from a typical king?

Zechariah describes a King who will come, not to inaugurate war but to bring peace. As a nation with a history of oppression, this is likely not the news that God's people are expecting to hear, for they want a king who will bring more than just peace. Yet this is just the type of king they need—a king who would deliver not just the remnant of Israel but the whole world from the yoke of evil and sin. The prophet Zechariah also describes this King as "righteous" and "victorious" (Zechariah 9:9), referencing the King's upright character and obedience along with His ability to save those who are in need of deliverance (Zechariah 9:10).

> Why might God's people have reason to rejoice at the coming King's humble arrival?

The deliverance that this King would bring is not one of military power and might. He would not come to overthrow government powers but to inaugurate a kingdom whose dominion would be over all the earth. This kingdom would come not through violence but through the humility of a servant Messiah and King.

> Why would Israel need a righteous and victorious king?

At the beginning of the passage, God's people are instructed to rejoice loudly and triumphantly in response to the coming of the King. His arrival warrants worship from all those who hear of his coming. Zechariah's prophecy is the heralding of our humble King and Messiah, Jesus Christ, who will come in humility and peace.

Mark it Up: New Testament Passage

Today, we will see that Jesus is the promised King whom Zechariah prophesied about. Read John 12:12–16 two or three times and annotate, or mark up, the text as you read. For tips and examples on annotating, see pages 188–199.

Highlight any words or phrases that point to Christ.

Make note of any attributes of God seen in the text.

Draw a box around the type of animal Jesus rides on when He comes into the city. Why is this significant?

Underline who the crowd says Jesus is at the end of verse 13.

Why might the disciples have been confused in verse 16?

JOHN 12:12–16

¹² The next day, when the large crowd that had come to the festival heard that Jesus was coming to Jerusalem, ¹³ they took palm branches and went out to meet him. They kept shouting:

"Hosanna!

Blessed is he who comes in the name of the Lord —the King of Israel!"

¹⁴ Jesus found a young donkey and sat on it, just as it is written:

¹⁵ Do not be afraid,

Daughter Zion. Look, your King is coming,

sitting on a donkey's colt.

¹⁶ His disciples did not understand these things at first. However, when Jesus was glorified, then they remembered that these things had been written about him and that they had done these things to him.

Make the Christ Connection

> Read Zechariah 9:9–12 and John 12:12–16.

From the prophet Zechariah, we learned of a humble and victorious King who would save and deliver His people. In John 12, we are introduced to this King by name, as Jesus Christ enters the city of Jerusalem riding on a donkey. In what is referred to as the triumphal entry, Jesus arrives on the same animal that Zechariah prophesied about in Zechariah 9:9.

As Jesus approaches, the crowd rejoices and shouts aloud at His coming, as was prophesied by Zechariah. Those gathered in the crowd truly believe that Jesus is a king (John 12:13). However, the crowd and even Jesus's disciples have yet to understand what kind of king Jesus is (John 12:16). As they shout "Hosanna," a plea for salvation, the crowd also waves palm branches, which are symbols of Jewish nationalism. The Israelites, who are suffering under the oppression of Rome, are calling out to Jesus to save them from the powers of the Roman Empire. Yet while Jesus is a king who is victorious and able to save, He will do so not by a sword but by surrendering to the will of the Father and dying on a cross.

> Read Philippians 2:5–8. How does Christ's humility bring salvation?

Jesus's humble and triumphal entry on a lowly animal symbolizes the way in which He will bring salvation. Philippians 2:6 tells us that even though Jesus is God, He did not use His deity as a means to be forceful and domineering. Instead, He humbled Himself and became a servant—a servant of God and servant to those around Him. In the ultimate act of humility, Jesus was obedient to death—a humiliating criminal's death on a cross. But through this humility, Jesus, the Messiah and King, proved that He is the victorious Savior foretold by the prophet Zechariah (Zechariah 9:9).

> Read Philippians 2:9–11. How will Christ's kingship ultimately be displayed?

Christ's humility does not mean that evil rulers and oppressive powers will always have the upper hand. While Zechariah's prophecy foretold Jesus's first coming, it also reminds us of Jesus's Second Coming. So too, Revelation 11:15 reminds us that Christ's reign over the kingdom of God will be global and eternal. Like Israel, we also wait for our King. In Revelation 7:9, a multitude from every tribe, tongue, and nation wave palm branches before Jesus, the Lamb of God, and shout aloud of His salvation, reflecting the scene in John 12:12–16. Though Jesus's first coming was one of humble obscurity, one day Jesus will return, and He will overthrow the powers of injustice that reign on earth. The time is coming when every knee will bow before Jesus, the King above all kings (Philippians 2:10–11).

> Write a prayer of gratitude for Christ's humility that brings salvation. Thank God that, one day, Jesus will overturn every evil and oppressive power on the earth.

Live it Out

> Read Zechariah 9:9 and John 12:12–16.

Because of Christ's humility, those who place their faith in Jesus benefit from the grandest act of sacrifice the world has ever known. Through His death, Jesus brings salvation to everyone who is willing to cry out "Hosanna!" and acknowledge Christ as their Lord and Savior. Like the people of Israel in the book of Zechariah, we, too, should shout aloud in triumphant praise for Jesus's humility that led to our deliverance from sin and death.

Jesus is our humble King. In His humility, Jesus demonstrated the attitude that members of God's kingdom should display. If Christ, who is God, humbled Himself to the lowest state by dying on a cross, how much more should we display the same humility? Christ, our servant Savior, did not come to be served but to serve. And we are called to be like Him.

One day, Jesus will come again—not as a lowly servant but as a conquering King. He who sees and knows the hearts of men will not leave evil unpunished. Though now we may still live under the effects of sin, injustice, and oppression, it will not be this way forever. Jesus's Second Coming will overturn the powers of darkness and free us, once and for all, from evil rulers both physical and spiritual.

Reflect on this week's verses as you answer the following questions.

> In what areas of your life can you demonstrate humility by serving those around you?

How are you encouraged by knowing that Jesus's return is imminent?

How did Christ's humility answer our need for salvation? Pause and thank God for Jesus, our servant Savior.

Christ, our servant Savior, did not come to be served but to serve.

Messianic Passages In Zechariah

ZECHARIAH 9:9

The Messiah entered Jerusalem on a donkey.

Referenced in Matthew 21:1–11, John 12:12–16

ZECHARIAH 11:12–13

The Messiah was sold.

Referenced in Matthew 26:15, 27:3–10

ZECHARIAH 12:10

The Messiah was pierced.

Referenced in John 19:34–37

ZECHARIAH 13:7

The Messiah's disciples were scattered.

Referenced in Matthew 26:31, 56

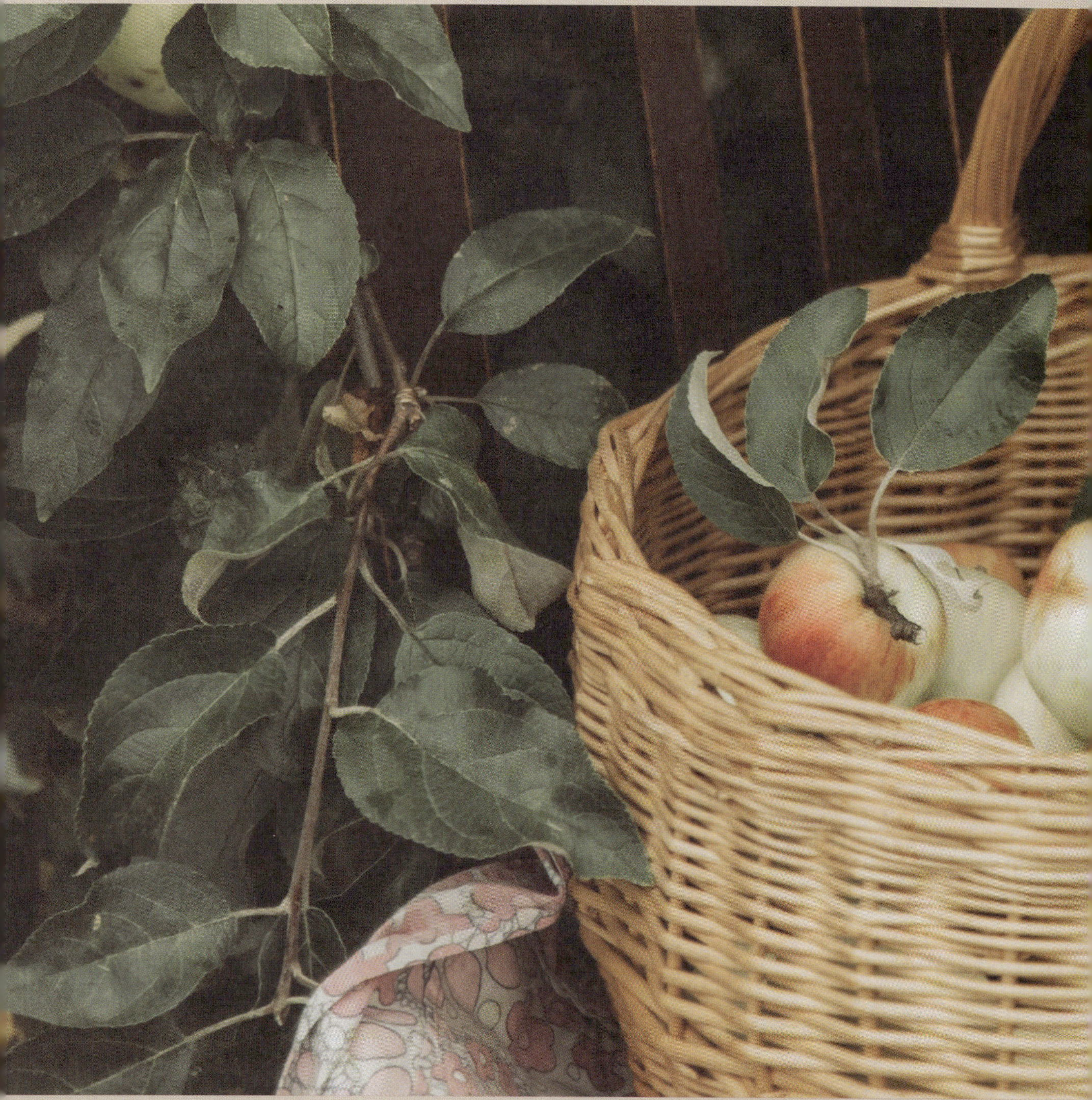

WEEK 50

Introduction

This week, we will read Malachi 3:1–5 and Mark 11:15–18 as we learn how God has come to His temple through Christ. In response, you will be led to gratitude in response to Christ's salvation and moved to share the good news of the gospel with others.

Mark it Up: Old Testament Passage

Today, we will read Malachi 3:1–5 and learn of God's promise to come to His temple and bring both refinement and judgment. Read the passage two or three times and annotate, or mark up, the text as you read. For tips and examples on annotating, see pages 188–199.

> Highlight any words or phrases that point to Christ.

> Make note of any attributes of God seen in the text.

> Underline any reference to the words "come" or "coming" in this passage.

> According to verse 1, who will come and where will he come to?
> Draw a box around the answers in the text.

> What will "the Messenger of the covenant" be like, according to verses 2–3?
> What will He do?

MALACHI 3:1–5

¹ "See, I am going to send my messenger, and he will clear the way before me. Then the Lord you seek will suddenly come to his temple, the Messenger of the covenant you delight in—see, he is coming," says the Lord of Armies. ² But who can endure the day of his coming? And who will be able to stand when he appears? For he will be like a refiner's fire and like launderer's bleach. ³ He will be like a refiner and purifier of silver; he will purify the sons of Levi and refine them like gold and silver. Then they will present offerings to the Lord in righteousness. ⁴ And the offerings of Judah and Jerusalem will please the Lord as in days of old and years gone by.

⁵ "I will come to you in judgment, and I will be ready to witness against sorcerers and adulterers; against those who swear falsely; against those who oppress the hired worker, the widow, and the fatherless; and against those who deny justice to the resident alien. They do not fear me," says the Lord of Armies.

Go Deeper

> Read Malachi 3:1–5.

Have you ever waited a long time for something that you were looking forward to? Maybe you had a vacation planned for the end of the year, and you spent each day in anticipation of that trip. Perhaps you longed to be married, and you waited years for God to bring you a spouse. Or maybe you have been pregnant and remember waiting in expectation for your little one to arrive. The people of Israel knew what it was like to wait a long time. God had promised Israel that He would send a Messiah who would defeat Israel's enemies and establish God's eternal kingdom (2 Samuel 7:10–13). But this promised Messiah still had not arrived.

The book of Malachi describes the time after the Exile in which the Israelites are waiting. They have returned to their land, and the temple has been rebuilt. But the Messiah has not yet arrived on the scene. This leaves the Israelites questioning whether God will do what He has promised. *Will God be faithful to His covenant? Will the Messiah come?* In Malachi 3:1–5, God assures His people that the Messiah will come, but it will be in a way that they might not expect.

In reading God's declaration in Malachi 3:1–5, it is important to consider the context of this passage and book. We have already noted that the Israelites are in a period of waiting, but in this time of waiting, God's people are not being fully obedient to Him. Infidelity is occurring among the people (Malachi 2:14), and the priests are not fulfilling their duties correctly (Malachi 1:11–13). Instead of following the sacrificial laws, the priests are allowing defiled food to be spilled on God's altar. Such actions reveal a lack of both reverence for the Lord and dedication to His law.

> Read Malachi 2:1–9. What have the priests done? What does God promise to do if they do not repent?

Because of the priests' disobedience, God promises to send judgment. A messenger will come to prepare the way, and then another Messenger, revealed to be God Himself, will come to His temple. His coming will involve refining fire for some and judgment for others. The metaphors in Malachi 3:2–3 of fire and bleach describe purification. For a gem to be refined, it must experience the flames of fire. For dirty clothes to be made clean, the filth must be taken away with harsh soap. In the same way, those who repent and turn to the Lord will experience a refinement that will purify their iniquities. But those who do not repent and remain in their wickedness will receive God's judgment (Malachi 3:5).

> **REPENT:**
> *The act of both confessing and turning away from sin in order to pursue obedience to God.*

> Why is repentance important? What does repentance look like?

Though God's people are waiting and in need of renewal, God promises to come to His people. Such a promise and proclamation leaves the Israelites with a choice. Will they remain in their disobedience? Or will they repent and return to the Lord? (Malachi 3:7). One decision will lead to just judgment, but the other will lead to righteous renewal.

> Consider God's invitation to return to Him. How does this invitation remain today, and how have you responded to this invitation?

Mark it Up: New Testament Passage

Today, we will read Mark 11:15–18 and learn how Jesus fulfills God's promise to come to His temple. Read the passage two or three times and annotate, or mark up, the text as you read. For tips and examples on annotating, see pages 188–199.

Highlight any words or phrases that point to Christ.

Make note of any attributes of God seen in the text.

Highlight in another color what Jesus does in verse 15.

According to the passage Jesus quotes in verse 17, what is God's house meant to be? Underline its purpose. What have the people made it be instead?

What is the priests' response to what Jesus does in this passage? According to verse 18, why do they respond this way?

MARK 11:15-18

¹⁵They came to Jerusalem, and he went into the temple and began to throw out those buying and selling. He overturned the tables of the money changers and the chairs of those selling doves, ¹⁶ and would not permit anyone to carry goods through the temple. ¹⁷ He was teaching them: "Is it not written, My house will be called a house of prayer for all nations? But you have made it a den of thieves!"

¹⁸ The chief priests and the scribes heard it and started looking for a way to kill him. For they were afraid of him, because the whole crowd was astonished by his teaching.

Make the Christ Connection

Read Malachi 3:1–5 and Mark 11:15–18.

In Malachi 3:1–5, God promised to come to His temple, and in Mark 11:15–18, we see this promise fulfilled in Jesus. This passage takes place after Jesus makes His triumphal entry into Jerusalem. After this event, Jesus goes to the temple and looks around, but He leaves because it is late. Before returning to the temple the next day, Jesus curses a barren fig tree (Mark 11:14). While this occurrence may seem unrelated to the surrounding text, it is important to note that the barren fig tree symbolizes the withered worship of the people. Israel—and their leaders in particular—are not being faithful in their worship and obedience to God; therefore, they are as barren as this fig tree.

We see an example of this wayward worship and disobedience when Jesus returns to the temple and sees that it is not being used as it should be. People are using the temple sacrifices for selfish gain through their buying and selling. Rather than treating the temple with reverence, they are viewing it as something that can benefit their greed. Not only this, but the buying and selling that occurs in the temple courtyard prevents Gentiles from being able to pray and worship in peace. Therefore, Jesus throws out the merchants and overturns the money changers' tables.

> Consider the importance of the temple and how the people were supposed to respond to God's temple. Why are Jesus's actions fair in light of the temple's significance?

Jesus's words in Mark 11:17 reveal the purpose of the temple: it is to be a house of prayer for *all* nations. But sadly, the people have made it a den of thieves. Similar to how the priests acted in Malachi's day, the people are not treating God's temple with the reverence it so deserves. Jesus's actions can be seen as judgment, as He condemns and clears out the greedy people. But His actions can also be seen as refinement, as cleansing the temple from sinful practices enables the temple to be used rightly and respectfully.

The response to Jesus's actions is mixed. The crowd is astonished, but the chief priests and scribes seek to kill Him. These leaders should have seen Jesus's actions as a divine act that points to God's authority (Mark 11:27–33). They should have agreed that the people's actions were wrong and supported Jesus's actions instead. They should have listened to the words of John the Baptist—the fulfillment of the messenger in Malachi 3:1 who prepared the way for the ultimate Messenger, Jesus—and repented. But they did not. Instead, they chose to set themselves against Jesus.

> How do you see people today respond in the same way as the religious leaders?

The religious leaders' actions sadly lead to their judgment. In fact, all those who do not repent and turn to Jesus will receive judgment when He comes again. However, those who do listen to Jesus, believe in Him, and repent from their sinful ways will be rescued from judgment. On the cross, Jesus took on the judgment all sinners deserve for their sin. Through His sacrifice, Jesus offers forgiveness for those who trust and believe in Him, resulting in their being rescued from punishment and purified of their sins.

> If you are not a believer, consider the salvation Jesus offers you. If you are a believer, consider the salvation you have received and pray a prayer of gratitude to the Lord in response.

Live it Out

> Read Malachi 3:1–5 and Mark 11:15–18.

Jesus has fulfilled God's promise to come to His temple, and surely He will come again, fulfilling God's promise of judgment. Such truth is sobering, but it reminds us of how important it is for those who do not know Jesus to repent and turn to Him before it is too late. God's coming judgment for sinners moves us to share the gospel with those around us in hopes that they will receive God's forgiveness and salvation. Knowing that Christ has taken on our judgment should lead us to gratitude and humility, motivating us to share with others the good news that the salvation we have received can be theirs, too.

While the truth of God's judgment is sobering, as believers, we can look forward to Christ's return with hope. Revelation 21 reminds us of what will come to pass after Jesus's return, promising us a world made new. There will be no more brokenness. There will be no more darkness. There will be no more troubles or pain. God's presence will be fully with His people. Our bodies will be fully renewed and restored, as we will be fully purified from all sin (1 Corinthians 15:42–49, 51–53). For all eternity, we will dwell with our Savior, singing His praises. So let us look ahead to this day with joy and hope, anticipating the return of the One who has redeemed us, renewed us, and restored us.

Reflect on this week's verses as you answer the following questions.

> How does the truth of future punishment for unrepentant sinners impact you?

How does Christ's return give you hope for the present?

In what ways can you live in light of Christ's imminent return?

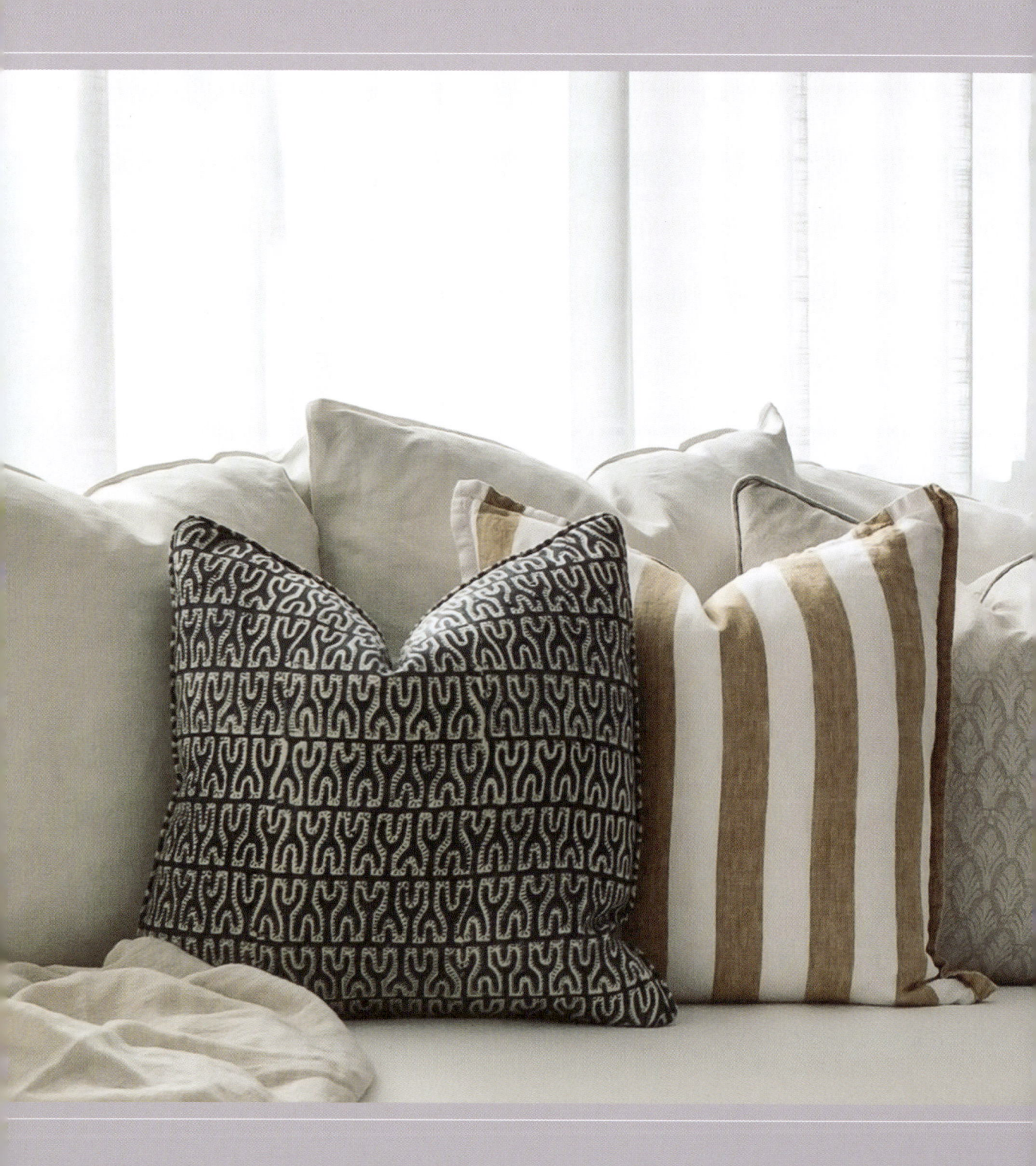

WEEK 51

Introduction

This week, we will return to the first pages of the Bible and read its words alongside the last pages of the Bible. By studying Genesis 2:8–9 and Revelation 22:1–3, we will see how Christ is the resolution of the whole biblical story—the One who restores us to the Tree of Life—and we will be encouraged to hope in the restoration He will bring when He returns.

Mark it Up: Old Testament Passage

Today, we will study Genesis 2:8–9, which will prepare us to see, later in the week, how Christ restores the goodness of God's creation and offers us eternal life. Read the passage multiple times and annotate, or mark up, the text as you read. For tips and examples on annotating, see pages 188–199.

Highlight any words or phrases that point to Christ.

Make note of any attributes of God seen in the text.

Circle instances of the word "tree" in the passage.

Underline the adjectives, or the words used to describe the different trees in this passage. Make note of the different purposes of each tree.

GENESIS 2:8-9

⁸ The Lord God planted a garden in Eden, in the east, and there he placed the man he had formed. ⁹ The Lord God caused to grow out of the ground every tree pleasing in appearance and good for food, including the tree of life in the middle of the garden, as well as the tree of the knowledge of good and evil.

Go Deeper

> Read Genesis 2:8–9.

Throughout this study, you have worked your way through the Old Testament, looking at different passages from Genesis to Malachi, discovering how Jesus is present on every page. But this week, to fully connect the dots, we are returning to Genesis. Back in the beginning of the biblical story, God created a good world (Genesis 1:31) and planted a garden full of abundance, goodness, and life.

> Look over Genesis 1. What does it mean that the creation was good? (For reference, see Genesis 1:10, 12, 18, 21, 25, 31.)

Because we live in a post-Fall world, it is almost impossible to imagine what the original creation was actually like. Were there no mosquitoes? Were all animals herbivores? There is no way of knowing exactly, but what we do know for sure is that God created the world exactly the way He wanted to. Everything was assigned a place in God's created world, everything had a purpose, everything was appropriately and joyfully working to accomplish that purpose, and most importantly, everything was completely dependent on God.

The world was good and exactly how God intended it, and He gave it potential to grow and to flourish. This is why the first humans were given the command to cultivate it and work it in order to produce fruit (Genesis 1:28, 2:15). They were also commanded to be fruitful themselves and produce offspring (Genesis 1:28). The first humans' job was to spread the goodness and abundance of the garden to the rest of the earth, but they were not to do this alone. They were invited to walk with God in this work, and in return, He would sustain them with everything they needed: trees that were good for food and the Tree of Life (Genesis 2:9).

> Read Genesis 3:22–23. Why were the humans removed from the garden?

The command to not eat from the Tree of the Knowledge of Good and Evil was predicated on the condition that if they did, they would die (Genesis 2:16–17). In Genesis 3:22–23, we see this consequence come to fruition. Adam and Eve eat the fruit, their eyes are opened, and they are introduced to the reality of sin and the reality of a life apart from God. Living forever in sin is not God's plan or desire for humanity, and it certainly is not good for humanity. So God casts them out of the garden and removes their access to the Tree of Life. It was not long before death reigned over the earth.

> Based on what you have learned so far in this study, how does God plan to redeem the plight of humanity found in Genesis 3?

Now, God could have abandoned creation to its destruction and death, but we know that is not what He does. Throughout this study, we have seen the stories of Abraham, David, and the nation of Israel. We have seen how they all point us to God's plan of redemption through Christ and the hope we have of complete restoration when Christ returns. The same is true for this story. From the very beginning, even as sin enters the world, we see evidence of God's plan of redemption that is ultimately fulfilled through Jesus Christ—a plan of redemption that is made complete in Revelation 22:1–3.

Mark it Up: New Testament Passage

Today, we read Revelation 22:1–3 and see how Jesus ushers in a garden city and restores humanity's access to the Tree of Life. Read the passage multiple times and annotate, or mark up, the text as you read. For tips and examples on annotating, see pages 188–199.

Highlight any words or phrases that point to Christ.

Make note of any attributes of God seen in the text.

Circle any references to the "city" in this passage. Look back at Revelation 21 and make note of references to the "city" in that chapter, as well.

Underline any words or phrases that describe the Tree of Life.

What words would you use to describe the garden city described in this passage?

REVELATION 22:1–3

¹ Then he showed me the river of the water of life, clear as crystal, flowing from the throne of God and of the Lamb ² down the middle of the city's main street. The tree of life was on each side of the river, bearing twelve kinds of fruit, producing its fruit every month. The leaves of the tree are for healing the nations, ³ and there will no longer be any curse. The throne of God and of the Lamb will be in the city, and his servants will worship him.

Make the Christ Connection

> Read Genesis 2:8–9 and Revelation 22:1–3.

Earlier this week, we looked at the very beginning of history, and today, we look at the very end. We see clearly through these passages what this entire study is intended to demonstrate—that Christ is the "the Alpha and the Omega, the beginning and the end" (Revelation 21:6).

> Read Revelation 21:1–7 along with Revelation 22:1–3. What comparisons between the garden of Eden and the New Jerusalem can you identify in these passages?

The garden was never intended to remain a mere garden. It was created with the potential to grow and flourish and develop into a city—a city fit for a King. Even after the Fall, God worked through His creation to make this promised garden city a reality. We see that the potential of Eden will be brought to full realization in the new creation, and the consequences of the Fall will be undone. Humanity will once again fully walk with, dwell with, and depend upon God. He will be their God, and they will worship Him alone.

Everything will once again be made good—mourning turned to rejoicing, pain and sorrow removed. At last, death will be no more—for the King "will freely give to the thirsty from the spring of the water of life" (Revelation 21:6). We see in Revelation 22 that this water of life comes from a river that flows down "from the throne of

God and of the Lamb" (Revelation 22:1). This river runs through the streets of the city, and on either side of this river of life is the Tree of Life. This is Eden worked and kept and brought to fruition as a city (Genesis 2:15)—only the city is not established by human hands but by the work of Christ.

> What is the significance of Jesus being referred to as "the Lamb" in this passage (Revelation 22:1, 3)?

Throughout the whole book of Revelation, the Apostle John, the author, describes Jesus as "the Lamb." This references what was said about Jesus by a different John—John the Baptist—who identified Christ as "the Lamb of God, who takes away the sins of the world" (John 1:29) when Jesus began His earthly ministry. We learned in week 11 (see *Christ in All of Scripture | Volume 1*) that this declaration is a reference to the Passover lamb from Exodus 12:1–13 and points us to Christ's sacrificial death on the cross. Through His death and resurrection, He took away the sins of the world and defeated death. And because of His work, as Revelation 22:3 explains, "there will no longer be any curse."

Christ's first coming, His death, and His resurrection inaugurated the reign of His kingdom. He then ascended to sit at the right hand of God on the heavenly throne, where He prepares for His Second Coming. On that day, heaven and earth will unite, God's throne will be established once and for all, the garden city will come to fruition, and all who trust in the Lamb for salvation will eat the fruit of the Tree of Life forever and ever. We, along with all of creation, eagerly await this day (Romans 8:19). In the words of the Apostle John, we say, "Amen! Come, Lord Jesus!" (Revelation 22:20).

> Pray and thank God for sending Christ to take our sins and for His promise to send Him again to fully establish His kingdom.

Live it Out

> Read Genesis 2:8–9 and Revelation 22:1–3.

Through this week's readings, we took a step back to look at the overarching story of Scripture. We have seen God's work from the first pages of the Bible to the last. And we have seen how, through Christ, He was—and will continue to be—faithful to bring the work He began in creation to completion when Christ returns.

Those first humans, and all after them, suffered the consequences of sin and rebellion through the curse of death—the result of their removal from the garden and the Tree of Life. But Christ took that curse upon Himself when He died on the cross (Galatians 3:13). Through His resurrection, He defeated the curse of death, and now we await His return, when He will remove sin and death once and for all and re-establish the garden—this time, as a city. The Tree of Life will be at the center, receiving its life source from the river that flows from the throne of God and Christ, the Lamb.

From the beginning to the end, we see Christ promised, proclaimed, and present. He connects the dots of this story on every page—from Genesis to Revelation.

Reflect on this week's verses as you answer the following questions.

> What remnants of God's good creation have you experienced in your own life? What effects of the Fall have you experienced in your own life?

How does the death and resurrection of Jesus provide you personally with hope for the future?

How has seeing Christ as the center and resolution of the biblical story encouraged you in your study of the Bible?

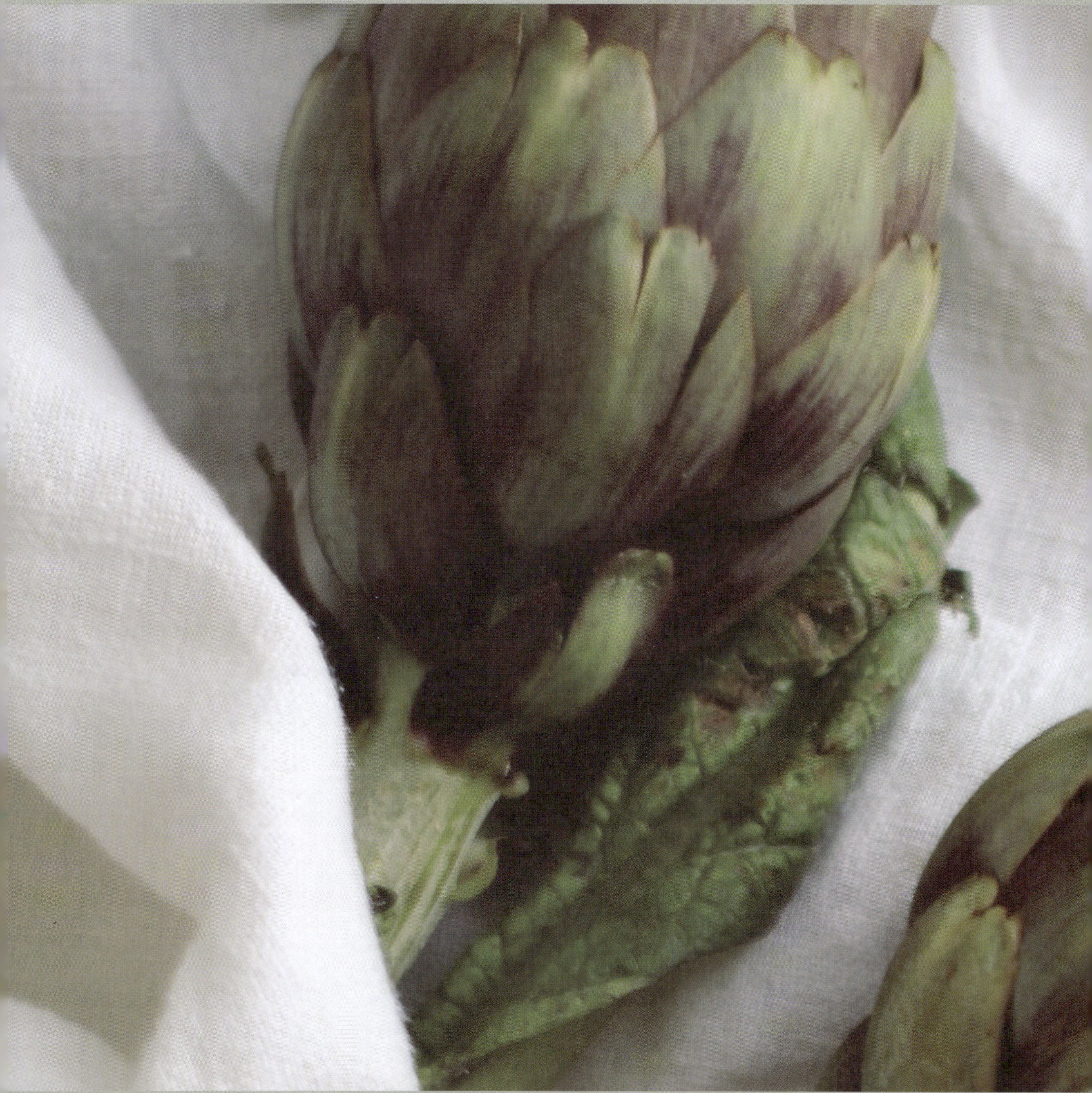

WEEK 52

Introduction

You have made it to the final week of this study, *Christ in All of Scripture*! In the coming days, you will have an opportunity to look back and reflect on all that God has shown you throughout the last fifty-one weeks of study. You will also be prompted to think about how to take what you have learned and apply it to your own Scripture reading moving forward.

Looking Back

You have probably heard the saying "practice makes perfect." While "perfect" might be an unrealistic bar to hit for anything, we can all testify to the fact that the more we practice something, the better we become at it. Some skills—which, at one time, might have felt daunting—now feel like second nature.

Take driving, for example. When first learning to drive, it can feel equal parts exhilarating and terrifying. New drivers may look for any opportunity to drive somewhere and are often hyperaware of everything they do. But with practice, driving eventually becomes reflexive.

Or think about learning to ride a bicycle. First, you learn to ride with training wheels on. But then, the training wheels come off, and you have to figure out how to stay upright without them. Many falls will likely ensue, but eventually, it will start to click, and a whole new world will seem to open up ahead of you.

So many of the skills we use throughout our day-to-day lives had to first be learned. In the same way, seeing Christ in all of Scripture is a skill that must be learned and then developed over time. The goal of this study has not been to make you an *expert* by the time you reach the end. Rather, the hope has been to provide you with tools you can now use to continue to develop this skill long after this study has been completed.

But before we look ahead to what comes next, it is worth pausing to look back on the ground you have covered. Using the prompts below, take some unhurried time to reflect on what God has shown you through this study.

> What are some of your biggest takeaways from *Christ in All of Scripture*?

_____

_____

_____

_____

_____

_____

What connections to Jesus did you see through this study that you had never noticed before?

How can seeing Christ in all of Scripture help us love Him more? How can it help us love Scripture more?

Use the space below to record any additional reflections you may have on what God taught you about Himself and His Word through this study. You may also choose to write out a short prayer, thanking God for all He has revealed to you and asking Him to help you continue to grow in love for Him and His Word.

Looking Ahead

As you finish *Christ in All of Scripture*, you might be intimidated by the prospect of continuing to do this kind of work on your own. Maybe this study has felt like having a guide next to you as you read Scripture. Maybe it has felt like having training wheels that you are now being asked to give up!

This is understandable. Again, seeing Christ in all of Scripture is a skill that, like all skills, takes time to develop. Plus, the Bible is a big book. When you think about it, this study has only covered a fraction of its passages. There are still many, many other parts of the Bible not covered in this study where we might struggle to see Jesus.

Here are some reminders and encouragements for you as you look ahead:

READ THE BIBLE WITH A SENSE OF PATIENT EXPECTANCY.

As Jesus said in Luke 24:44–47, the Old Testament points toward Him. In John 5:39, He said that the Scriptures—by which He referred to the entire Old Testament—testify about Him. And Paul tells his protégé Timothy that "all Scripture is inspired by God and is profitable for teaching, for rebuking, for correcting, for training in righteousness" (2 Timothy 3:16).

Imagine you are digging for buried treasure in an open field. After hours of digging, you are tired and hot. Yet while you might take breaks, you do not quit because you know for a fact that there is treasure buried in this field. This knowledge keeps you going when you might have been tempted to quit. In a similar way, the verses above remind us that there is a treasure—Christ—to be found in all of Scripture. It might take more digging to find Him in some passages than in others. But He is there, and this knowledge ought to sustain us when we do not see Him in a passage right away.

> Though Christ is present in all of Scripture, it is not always in the same way.

KNOW WHAT TO LOOK FOR.

Though Christ is present in all of Scripture, it is not always in the same way. For example, you might read Micah 5:2, which speaks of a future ruler being born in Bethlehem, and conclude—correctly—that this is ultimately a reference to Jesus's birth in Bethlehem (Matthew 2:1–6). This is a prediction about Jesus that came true.

But we are not only looking for predictions about Jesus when we read the Old Testament. As we learned in the very first week of this study, we are also looking for how roles, problems, symbols, themes, promises, and people point to Him. So, as we read the Bible, we should regularly ask questions like:

- What *roles* do I see in this text (e.g., king, prophet, priest, etc.)? How does Jesus perfectly fill these roles?

- What *problems* are present in this passage (e.g., brokenness, pain, death)? How does Jesus solve these problems?

- What *symbols* do I see in this passage that prefigure Jesus in some way? For example, how might the instructions on various sacrifices in Leviticus 1–7 help us appreciate Jesus offering Himself as a sacrifice on the cross?

- What *themes* do I see in this passage that in some way ultimately culminate in Christ? In the Old Testament, for example, we see that God is merciful and that He judges sin. How does Jesus demonstrate both God's mercy and judgment?

- What *promises* from God do I see present in this passage? Is a promise being made? Does a prior promise inform what is happening? And how does Jesus fulfill this promise?

- In what ways do the *people* in this passage point to Jesus? Remember that people can point to Jesus in positive or negative ways. For example, Joseph forgiving his brothers who had wronged him draws our attention to Jesus, who likewise extends forgiveness to sinners. On the other hand, Israel's rebellion against God in the wilderness contrasts sharply with Jesus, who was obedient to God in the wilderness (Matthew 4:1–11).

You may find it helpful to revisit the section "How to See Christ in All of Scripture" on page 188 for more information on looking for these elements as you read.

FAMILIARIZE YOURSELF WITH THE BIBLE.

In other words, read it a lot! Our prayer is that this study has given you many tools for reading the Bible well. But there is also no substitute for simply spending time in God's Word and becoming deeply familiar with it.

Think of it this way: How many times have you rewatched a movie or reread a novel only to catch details you missed the first time around? As you become more familiar with that movie or book, you will be better prepared to make connections between the story's various components. You will start to see the foreshadowing behind a seemingly simple line of dialogue. You will catch how characters are meant to contrast with each other. The significance of certain details will start to become apparent.

Similarly, the more time you spend reading the Bible, the better prepared you will be to make the kind of connections we have been making throughout this study. Even if you are not sure *why* certain details or people are significant in a particular passage, there is tremendous value in observing that they are there. As your familiarity with the Bible grows, you will place yourself in a position to one day understand the significance of those details.

READ THE BIBLE WITH OTHERS!

You can do this in a variety of ways. Maybe you decide to read through a book of the Bible with two or three other people and discuss what you're learning together. Or maybe each of you are reading separate parts of the Bible but choose to gather and share what you are all reading. Maybe you find a pastor or more spiritually mature Christian with whom you can discuss your questions about the Bible. Whatever form it takes, bring other believers into your study of Scripture. You will have a greater chance of seeing Christ in all of Scripture when others are helping you look for Him.

As this study comes to a close, take some time to answer the following reflection questions:

> Moving forward, how might the way you read the Bible be impacted as a result of this study?

_____

_____

_____

_____

_____

Is there a passage or book of the Bible that you have struggled to see Christ in? How might the tools found throughout this study aid you in seeing Him there?

What questions or concerns do you have about implementing the practices found in this study?

Who can come alongside you as you read the Bible?
Who can help you in your efforts to see Christ in all of Scripture?

Jesus saved us from the wrath
that our sins deserve
at great cost to Himself.

Remembering the Purpose

Why does all of this matter? Why is it so important to see Christ in all of Scripture?

There are many answers that can be given in response to these questions. But at the end of the day, we do so to know Jesus. Jesus saved us from the wrath that our sins deserve at great cost to Himself. He rose from the grave, conquering death itself. He ascended to heaven, where He currently reigns as King. And one day, He will come back, rid the world of every last trace of sin, and live with us forever.

We look for Christ in all of Scripture to remind ourselves of how He gave everything to make us His own. And we look for Him to remind ourselves that this world and this life are not all there is. There is a future beyond death, and it is with Him. Seeing Christ in all of Scripture helps us grasp these ultimate realities as we walk with Him through this life on our way home.

> We look for Christ in all of Scripture to remind ourselves of how He gave everything to make us His own.

Volume 4 Conclusion

Congratulations! If you have reached this page, that means you have completed the *Christ in All of Scripture* study set. In this fourth and final volume, you have read, annotated, and considered many passages from across the Old and New Testaments. In doing so, you have continued to see how all of Scripture points us to Jesus Christ.

We began this fourth volume with God's promise to shepherd His people—a promise that is ultimately fulfilled in Jesus Christ, our Good Shepherd. From there, we looked at how subsequent prophetic books point ahead to Christ in many other ways. Ultimately, we have seen how Jesus is the hope of the world.

Our hope is that this study has helped you grow in your love for God. And we pray that as you continue to study God's Word, your love for Him will only increase. May we rejoice in His glorious plan of redemption, which is on display from the first pages of Genesis to the final chapters of Revelation. And may we ultimately worship Christ for all He has done on our behalf. He is the main character of the story. And so, let us continue to commit ourselves to seeing His fingerprints on every page.

You can find all volumes of Christ in All of Scripture—*along with many more resources to equip you in your study of God's Word—at www.thedailygraceco.com.*

Jesus is the hope of the world.

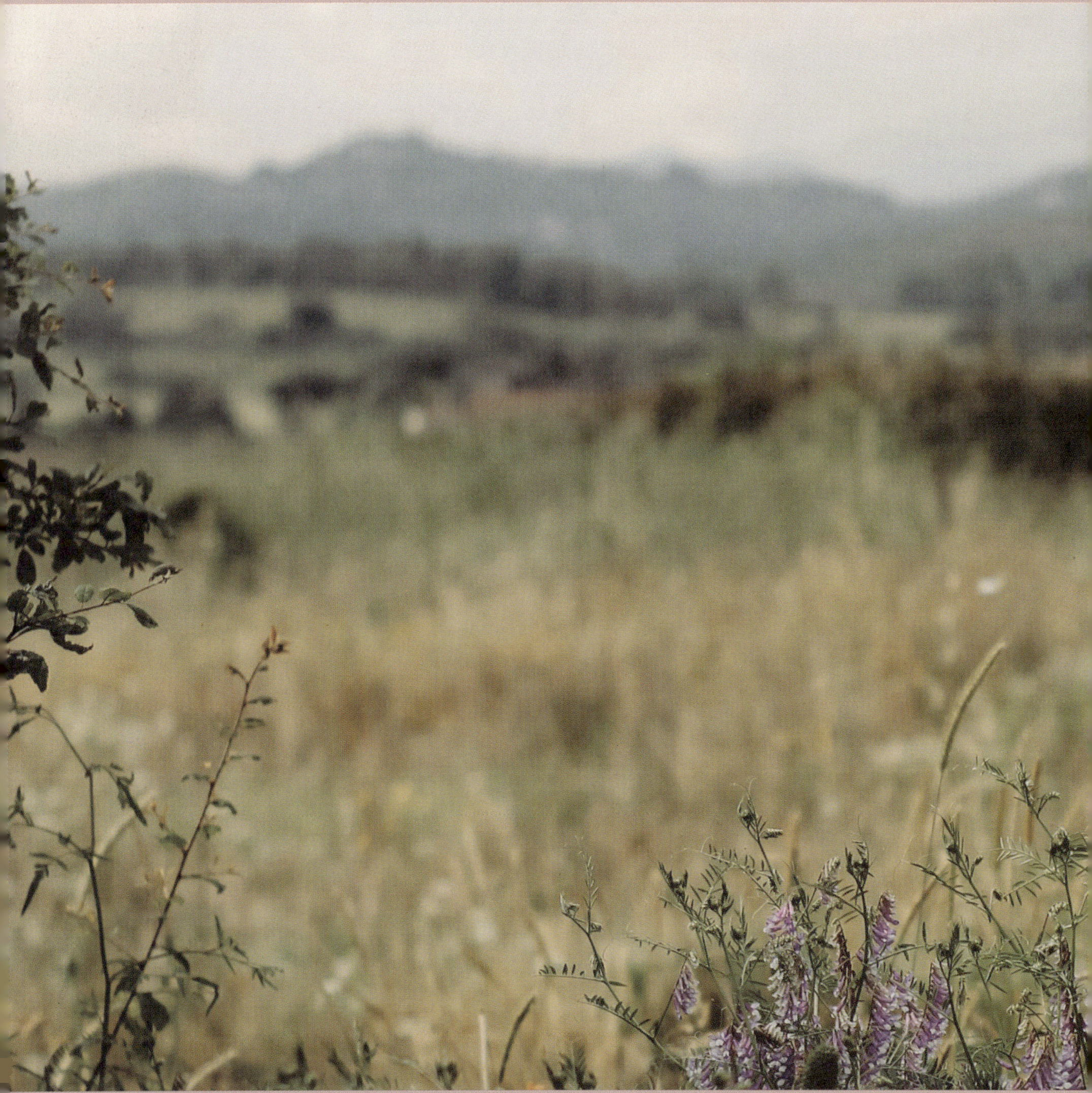

Appendix

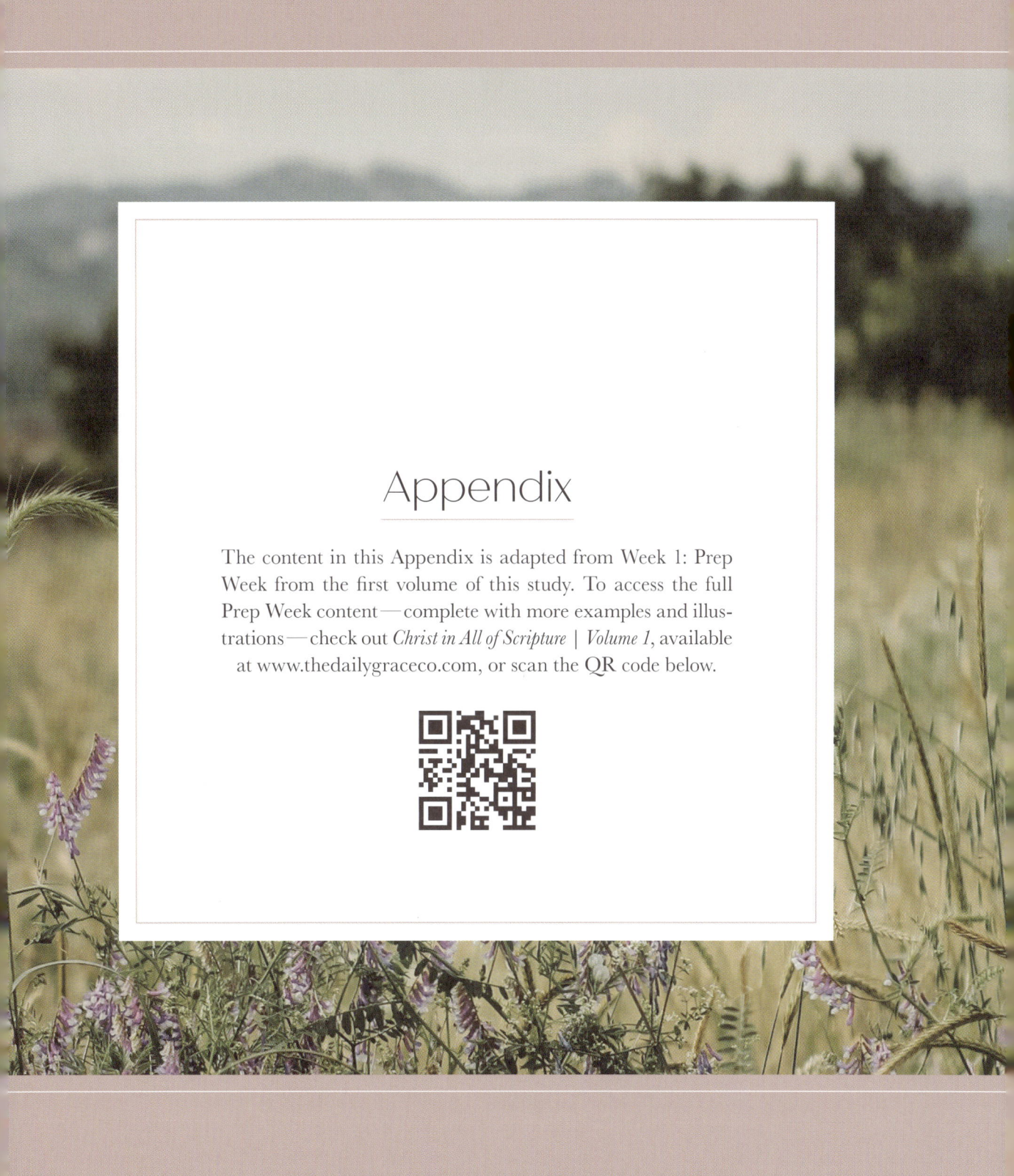

The content in this Appendix is adapted from Week 1: Prep Week from the first volume of this study. To access the full Prep Week content—complete with more examples and illustrations—check out *Christ in All of Scripture | Volume 1*, available at www.thedailygraceco.com, or scan the QR code below.

APPENDIX A

How to See Christ in All of Scripture

The study you hold in your hands centers on how we can find Christ in all of Scripture. But practically, how can we do so? The chart below describes seven elements you can look for in each passage—along with examples from the story of Noah in Genesis 6–9—that will point you in the right direction as you journey through Scripture. You may not find each of these elements in every passage you study, but often, one or more will be present, pointing you to Jesus Christ—even in the most unexpected places.

WHAT TO LOOK FOR	EXAMPLE (FROM GENESIS 6–9)
Roles: Positions seen throughout Scripture that are filled perfectly by Christ	There are many roles in the Old Testament that find their fulfillment in Christ. We can see this specifically in the roles of prophets, priests, and kings—three roles which Jesus perfectly fulfilled through His life, death, resurrection, and ascension into heaven. But there are more than just these. For example, Noah plays the role of a leader in Genesis 6–9 as he leads his family to salvation through the ark, just as Christ leads His people to salvation through His death and resurrection.
Problems: Examples of sin, brokenness, hurt, failure, or any other problems that are solved only through Christ	*See Genesis 6:5.* The human heart is evil, and wickedness fills the earth. This problem can only be solved through Christ, who is able to transform the hearts of humanity.
Symbols: Images or actions that predict an aspect of Christ's person or work	*See Genesis 7:23.* Only those who entered the ark were saved from God's judgment, just like only those who are in Christ will be saved from eternal judgment.

WHAT TO LOOK FOR	EXAMPLE (FROM GENESIS 6–9)
Themes: Concepts that repeat throughout Scripture and find their resolution in Christ	*See Genesis 9:1–7.* In these verses, God makes a covenant with Noah and his family that resembles the covenant made with Adam and Eve in Genesis 1:28–30. Covenants—or God's promises to His people—are a theme throughout Scripture. Through Christ, God's new covenant is established; therefore, this theme is ultimately resolved through Him.
Promises: Specific words of God that offer assurance of His faithfulness and are fulfilled in Christ	*See Genesis 9:15–16.* God promises to remember His covenant with Noah and not destroy humanity again. This promise finds its fulfillment in the coming of Christ, who makes a way for humanity to be saved and redeemed.
People: Figures throughout Scripture who point to Christ—sometimes through their success and faithfulness but, more often, through their failure to live up to their calling, thus pointing to Christ's perfection	*See Genesis 6:9 and 9:18–27.* Noah was righteous, found favor with God, and walked with Him, and God used Noah to save his family. But Noah was not perfect, as evidenced by his sin after the flood in Genesis 9:18–27. Noah could not change his own heart or the hearts of the people. This points to humanity's need for a Savior. Thankfully, Jesus is a true and better Noah. He is able to deliver people from judgment and transform their hearts.
Predictions: Passages that speak about future events that find their ultimate fulfillment in Christ	Such predictions are found mostly in the prophetic books of the Old Testament, so there is not an example from Genesis 6–9. *Examples include: Isaiah 9:6, Hosea 1:11.*

APPENDIX B

The Attributes of God

Another way we can see Christ in all of Scripture is by identifying and studying the attributes of God. These are the traits that are true of God throughout all time and history. And because our God is a triune God—three in one—these attributes are true of all three members of the Trinity: Father, Son, and Holy Spirit. As you work through this study, you may find it helpful to bookmark this page and come back to it often as you seek to discover glimpses and echoes of Christ's character and work in every passage you study.

Eternal
God has no beginning and no end. He always was, always is, and always will be.
HAB. 1:12 / REV. 1:8 / ISA. 41:4

Faithful
God is incapable of anything but fidelity. He is loyally devoted to His plan and purpose.
2 TIM. 2:13 / DEUT. 7:9 / HEB. 10:23

Good
God is pure; there is no defilement in Him. He is unable to sin, and all He does is good.
GEN. 1:31 / PS. 34:8 / PS. 107:1

Gracious
God is kind, giving us gifts and benefits we do not deserve.
2 KINGS 13:23 / PS. 145:8 / ISA. 30:18

Holy
God is undefiled and unable to be in the presence of defilement. He is sacred and set-apart.
REV. 4:8 / LEV. 19:2 / HAB. 1:13

Incomprehensible
God is high above and beyond human understanding. He is unable to be fully known.
PS. 145:3 / ISA. 55:8-9 / ROM. 11:33-36

Immutable
God does not change. He is the same yesterday, today, and tomorrow.
1 SAM. 15:29 / ROM. 11:29 / JAMES 1:17

Infinite
God is limitless. He exhibits all of His attributes perfectly and boundlessly.
ROM. 11:33-36 / ISA. 40:28 / PS. 147:5

Jealous
God is desirous of receiving the praise and affection He rightly deserves.
EXOD. 20:5 / DEUT. 4:23-24 / JOSH. 24:19

Just

God governs in perfect justice. He acts in accordance with justice. In Him, there is no wrongdoing or dishonesty.

ISA. 61:8 / DEUT. 32:4 / PS. 146:7-9

Loving

God is eternally, enduringly, steadfastly loving and affectionate. He does not forsake or betray His covenant love.

JOHN 3:16 / EPH. 2:4-5 / 1 JOHN 4:16

Merciful

God is compassionate, withholding from us the wrath that we deserve.

TITUS 3:5 / PS. 25:10 / LAM. 3:22-23

Omnipotent

God is all-powerful; His strength is unlimited.

MATT. 19:26 / JOB 42:1-2 / JER. 32:27

Omnipresent

God is everywhere; His presence is near and permeating.

PROV. 15:3 / PS. 139:7-10 / JER. 23:23-24

Omniscient

God is all-knowing; there is nothing unknown to Him.

PS. 147:4 / I JOHN 3:20 / HEB. 4:13

Patient

God is long-suffering and enduring. He gives ample opportunity for people to turn toward Him.

ROM. 2:4 / 2 PET. 3:9 / PS. 86:15

Self-Existent

God was not created but exists by His power alone.

PS. 90:1-2 / JOHN 1:4 / JOHN 5:26

Self-Sufficient

God has no needs and depends on nothing, but everything depends on God.

ISA. 40:28-31 / ACTS 17:24-25 / PHIL. 4:19

Sovereign

God governs over all things; He is in complete control.

COL. 1:17 / PS. 24:1-2 / 1 CHRON. 29:11-12

Truthful

God is our measurement of what is fact. By Him we are able to discern true and false.

JOHN 3:33 / ROM. 1:25 / JOHN 14:6

Wise

God is infinitely knowledgeable and is judicious with His knowledge.

ISA. 46:9-10 / ISA. 55:9 / PROV. 3:19

Wrathful

God stands in opposition to all that is evil. He enacts judgment according to His holiness, righteousness, and justice.

PS. 69:24 / JOHN 3:36 / ROM. 1:18

As you begin annotating, remember that we do not expect you to annotate every passage perfectly.

Annotation Examples and Tips

Each week of this study provides you with the opportunity to annotate two passages of Scripture—one from the Old Testament and one from the New Testament. In doing so, you will grow in your ability to study Scripture and make Christ connections in each passage you encounter. However, if the idea of annotation seems intimidating to you, do not fret! We have provided some helpful examples below, showing you what this might look like in a few different passages of Scripture.

As you begin annotating, remember that we do not expect you to annotate every passage perfectly. Additionally, if you come across an annotation prompt that challenges you or leaves you with more questions than answers, that's okay! You may find it helpful to look at the surrounding context of that passage (i.e., the verses or chapters that come just before and just after it). And at times, you may simply jot down your questions to come back to later in the week.

TIPS FOR ANNOTATING A PASSAGE

1. Look up key words in a concordance to identify cross-references.

2. Read the surrounding context of the passage (i.e., the verses or chapters that come before or after it) to aid your understanding.

3. As you look for connections to Jesus, use highlighters and/or write notes and questions in the margins.

4. If it is difficult to see the connection to Jesus, that's okay! Pray, read the verses surrounding the passage, and be patient as you read. Each week, the commentary will help you make those connections.

5. In addition to making notes in the margins, there will be space for you to jot down notes underneath each annotation prompt. If you don't have notes, feel free to leave those spaces blank!

EXAMPLE ANNOTATION 1

PSALM 23

The Good Shepherd

A psalm of David.

[1] The (LORD) is my shepherd; → *provider / protector*

I have what I need.

[2] (He) lets me lie down in green pastures;

(he) leads me beside quiet waters.

[3] (He) renews my life; → *merciful*

sovereign → (he) leads me along the right paths

for (his) name's sake.

[4] Even when I go through the darkest valley,

I fear no danger,

194

Circle the words that describe God or are from God.
Underline the actions of God.
Make note of where you see His attributes.

for you are with me;   *loving*

your rod and your staff — they comfort me.

⁵ You prepare a table before me   *gracious*

in the presence of my enemies;

you anoint my head with oil;

my cup overflows.

good   ⁶ Only goodness and faithful love will pursue me   *faithful*

all the days of my life,

and I will dwell in the house of the L ORD   *omnipresent*

as long as I live.

EXAMPLE ANNOTATION 2

PSALM 2

Coronation of the Son

Problem (rebellion) ←

¹ Why do the nations rage

and the peoples plot in vain?

² The kings of the earth take their stand,

and the rulers conspire together

against the LORD and his Anointed One:

³ "Let's tear off their chains

and throw their ropes off of us."

⁴ The one enthroned in heaven laughs;

the LORD ridicules them.

⁵ Then he speaks to them in his anger

and terrifies them in his wrath:

⁶ "I have installed my king → *People (King David)*

on Zion, my holy mountain."

⁷ I will declare the LORD's decree.

He said to me, "You are my Son; ⟶ *2 Samuel 7:14*
Mark 1:11
today I have become your Father. *Hebrews 1:5*

⁸ Ask of me,

Promise ⟵ and I will make the nations your inheritance
(Abrahamic covenant)

and the ends of the earth your possession.

⁹ You will break them with an iron scepter;

you will shatter them like pottery."

¹⁰ So now, kings, be wise;

receive instruction, you judges of the earth.

¹¹ Serve the Lord with reverential awe

and rejoice with trembling.

¹² Pay homage to the Son or he will be angry

and you will perish in your rebellion,

for his anger may ignite at any moment.

All who take refuge in him are happy.

In Christ, we find refuge.

Appendix C: Annotation Examples and Tips / 197

EXAMPLE ANNOTATION 3

Titus 2:14
Hebrews 9:15

Promise
(Redemption through
faith in Jesus)

Problem (Sin)

1 PETER 1:18-19

Jesus's blood
secures our
redemption

[18] For you know that you were redeemed from your empty way of life inherited from your ancestors, not with perishable things like silver or gold, [19] but with the precious blood of Christ, like that of an unblemished and spotless lamb.

Theme
(sacrifice)

Exodus 12
Isaiah 53:7
John 1:29

Highlight any words or phrases that point to Christ.

Make note of any attributes of God seen in the text.

Underline any words that point to the theme of sacrifice.
Where else do we see this in Scripture?

Circle any words or phrases that show Jesus's connection to sacrifice.

The Metanarrative of Scripture

In order to see Christ in all of Scripture, this study makes connections between the Old and New Testaments each week. In order to understand these connections, it is necessary to read the entire Bible through the lens of the metanarrative of Scripture—the four-part, overarching story of the Bible.

CREATION

In the beginning, God created the universe. He made the world and everything in it. He created humans in His own image to be His representatives on the earth.

FALL

The first humans, Adam and Eve, disobeyed God by eating from the fruit of the Tree of Knowledge of Good and Evil. Their disobedience impacted the whole world. The punishment for sin is death, and because of Adam's original sin, all humans are sinful and condemned to death.

REDEMPTION

God sent His Son to become a human and redeem His people. Jesus Christ lived a sinless life but died on the cross to pay the penalty for sin. He resurrected from the dead and ascended into heaven. All who put their faith in Jesus are saved from death and freely receive the gift of eternal life.

RESTORATION

One day, Jesus Christ will come again and restore all that sin destroyed. He will usher in a new heaven and new earth where all who trust in Him will live eternally with glorified bodies in the presence of God.

What is *the* Gospel?

Thank you for reading and enjoying this study with us! We are abundantly grateful for the Word of God, the instruction we glean from it, and the ever-growing understanding it provides for us of God's character. We are also thankful that Scripture continually points to one thing in innumerable ways: the gospel.

We remember our brokenness when we read about the fall of Adam and Eve in the garden of Eden (Genesis 3), where sin entered into a perfect world and maimed it. We remember the necessity that something innocent must die to pay for our sin when we read about the atoning sacrifices in the Old Testament. We read that we have all sinned and fallen short of the glory of God (Romans 3:23) and that the penalty for our brokenness, the wages of our sin, is death (Romans 6:23). We all need grace and mercy, but most importantly, we all need a Savior.

We consider the goodness of God when we realize that He did not plan to leave us in this dire state. We see His promise to buy us back from the clutches of sin and death in Genesis 3:15. And we see that promise accomplished with Jesus Christ on the cross. Jesus Christ knew no sin yet became sin so that we might become righteous through His sacrifice (2 Corinthians 5:21). Jesus was tempted in every way that we are and lived sinlessly. He was reviled yet still yielded Himself for our sake, that we may have life abundant in Him. Jesus lived the perfect life that we could not live and died the death that we deserved.

The gospel is profound yet simple. There are many mysteries in it that we will never understand this side of heaven, but there is still overwhelming weight to its implications in this life. The gospel tells of our sinfulness and God's goodness and a gracious gift that compels a response. We are saved by grace through faith, which means that we rest with faith in the grace that Jesus Christ displayed on the cross (Ephesians 2:8–9). We cannot save ourselves from our brokenness or do any amount of good works to merit God's favor. Still, we can have faith that what Jesus accomplished in His death, burial, and resurrection was more than enough for our salvation and our eternal delight. When we accept God, we are commanded to die to ourselves and our sinful desires and live a life worthy of the calling we have received (Ephesians 4:1). The gospel compels us to be sanctified, and in so doing, we are conformed to the likeness of Christ Himself. This is hope. This is redemption. This is the gospel.

GENESIS 3:15

I will put hostility between you and the woman, and between your offspring and her offspring. He will strike your head, and you will strike his heel.

ROMANS 3:23

For all have sinned and fall short of the glory of God.

ROMANS 6:23

For the wages of sin is death, but the gift of God is eternal life in Christ Jesus our Lord.

2 CORINTHIANS 5:21

He made the one who did not know sin to be sin for us, so that in him we might become the righteousness of God.

EPHESIANS 2:8-9

For you are saved by grace through faith, and this is not from yourselves; it is God's gift—not from works, so that no one can boast.

EPHESIANS 4:1-3

Therefore I, the prisoner in the Lord, urge you to walk worthy of the calling you have received, with all humility and gentleness, with patience, bearing with one another in love, making every effort to keep the unity of the Spirit through the bond of peace.

BIBLIOGRAPHY

Baldwin, Joyce G. *Daniel: An Introduction and Commentary*. Vol. 23 of Tyndale Old Testament Commentaries. Downers Grove, IL: InterVarsity Press, 1978.

Baldwin, Joyce G. *Haggai, Zechariah and Malachi: An Introduction and Commentary*. Vol. 28 of Tyndale Old Testament Commentaries. Downers Grove, IL: InterVarsity Press, 1972.

Barnett, Paul. *John: The Shepherd King*. Reading the Bible Today Series. Sydney South, NSW: Aquila Press, 2011.

Blue, J. Ronald. "Habakkuk." In *The Bible Knowledge Commentary: An Exposition of the Scriptures by Dallas Seminary Faculty*. Wheaton, IL: Victor Books, 1985.

Blum, Edwin A., and Trevin Wax, eds. *CSB Study Bible*. Nashville, TN: Holman Bible Publishers, 2017.

Boa, Kenneth, and William Kruidenier. Romans. Vol. 6. Holman New Testament Commentary. Nashville, TN: Broadman & Holman Publishers, 2000.

Bock, Darrell L. *Luke*. The NIV Application Commentary. Grand Rapids, MI: Zondervan, 1996.

Carson, D. A. *The Gospel according to John*. The Pillar New Testament Commentary. Grand Rapids, MI: William B. Eerdmans Publishing Company, 1991.

Carson, D. A., ed. *NIV Biblical Theology Study Bible*. Grand Rapids, MI: Zondervan, 2018.

Chen, Diane G. *Luke: A New Covenant Commentary*. New Covenant Commentary Series. Eugene, OR: Cascade Books, 2017.

Dial, Audrey, and Jennie Heideman, Helen Hummel, Alli McDougal, and Jana White, eds. *The Bible Handbook: A Book-by-Book Guide to the Entire Bible*. Spring, TX: The Daily Grace Co., 2024.

Edwards, James R. *The Gospel according to Mark*. The Pillar New Testament Commentary. Grand Rapids, MI: William B. Eerdmans Publishing Co., 2002.

Hubbard, David Allan. *Hosea: An Introduction and Commentary*. United Kingdom: InterVarsity Press, 2015.

Hubbard, David A. *Joel and Amos: An Introduction and Commentary*. Vol. 25 of Tyndale Old Testament Commentaries. Downers Grove, IL: InterVarsity Press, 1989.

Longman III, Tremper. *How to Read Genesis*. Westmont, IL: IVP Academic, 2005.

Matthews, Victor Harold, and Mark W. Chavalas and John H. Walton. *The IVP Bible Background Commentary: Old Testament*. Downers Grove, IL: InterVarsity Press, 2000. Electronic edition.

Middleton, J. Richard. *A New Heaven and a New Earth: Reclaiming Biblical Eschatology*. Grand Rapids, MI: Baker Publishing Group, 2014.

Morris, Leon. *The Gospel according to Matthew*. The Pillar New Testament Commentary. Grand Rapids, MI: William B. Eerdmans Publishing Co., 1992.

Morris, Leon. *Luke: An Introduction and Commentary*. Grand Rapids, MI: William B. Eerdmans Publishing Company, 1988.

Peterson, David G. *The Acts of the Apostles*. The Pillar New Testament Commentary. Grand Rapids, MI: William B. Eerdmans Publishing Company, 2009.

Platt, David. *Exalting Jesus in Matthew*. Christ-Centered Exposition Commentary. Nashville, TN: Holman Reference, 2013.

Redmond, Eric, and Bill Curtis and Ken Fentress. *Exalting Jesus in Jonah, Micah, Nahum, Habakkuk*. Christ-Centered Exposition Commentary. Nashville, TN: Holman Reference, 2016.

Stott, John R. W. *The Message of Acts*. The Bible Speaks Today. Downers Grove, IL: InterVarsity Press, 1990.

Stuart, Douglas K. *Hosea–Jonah*. Grand Rapids, MI: Zondervan, 2014.

Taylor, John B. *Ezekiel: An Introduction and Commentary*. Vol. 22 of Tyndale Old Testament Commentaries. Downers Grove, IL: InterVarsity Press, 1969.

Weber, Stuart K. *Matthew*. Vol. 1 of Holman New Testament Commentary. Nashville, TN: Broadman & Holman Publishers, 2000.

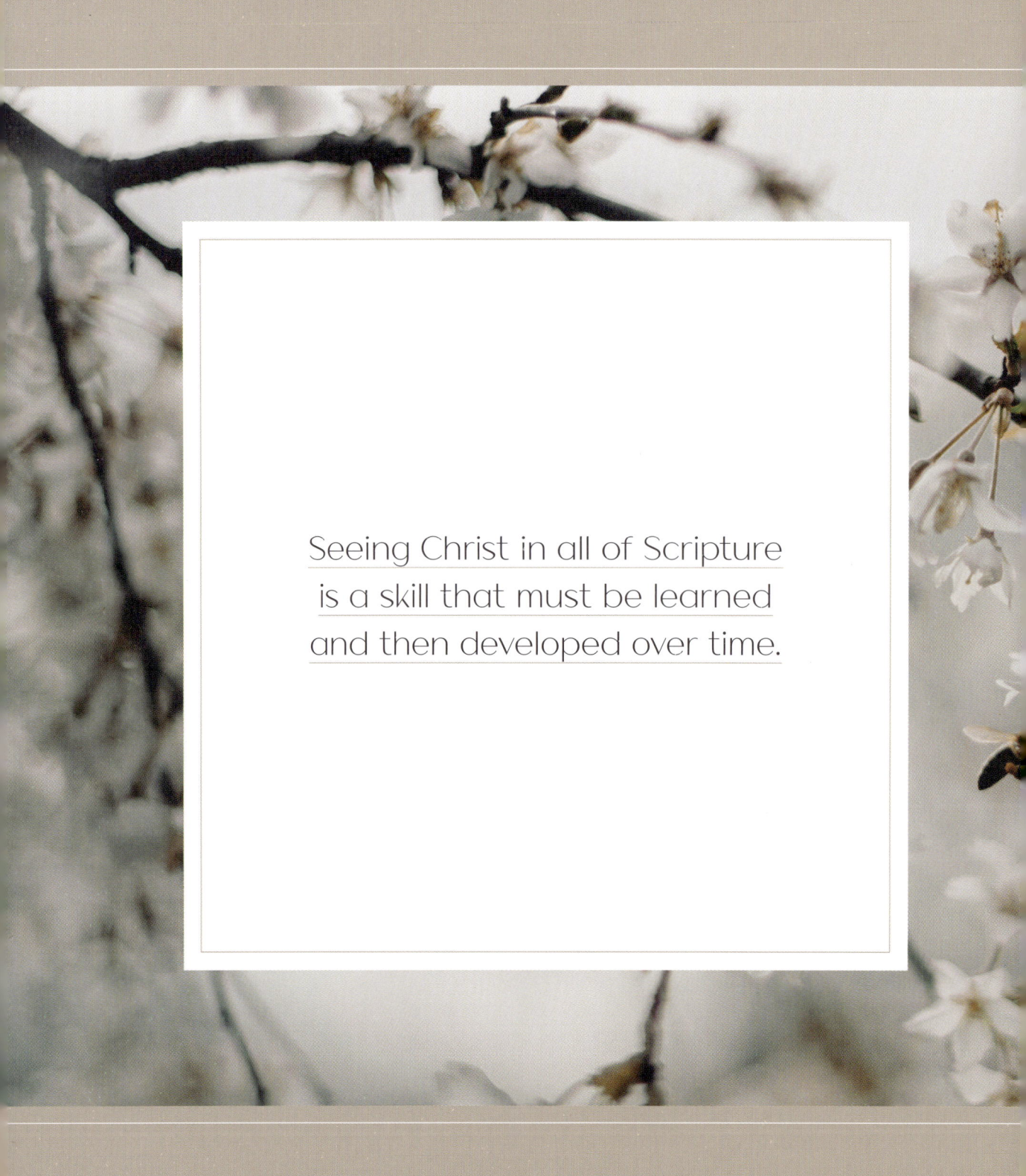

Seeing Christ in all of Scripture is a skill that must be learned and then developed over time.

Index

OLD TESTAMENT

Genesis

1	166
1:2	79
1:10	166
1:12	166
1:18	166
1:21	166
1:25	166
1:28	166
1:31	166
2:8–9	163, 164, 165, 166, 170, 172
2:9	166
2:15	166, 171
2:16–17	167
2:24	68
3	167
3:15	90
3:22–23	167
6–9	188, 189
6:5	188
6:9	189
7:23	188
9:1–7	189
9:15–16	189
9:18–27	189

Exodus

12:1–13	171
24:6–7	24
35:30–35	79

Leviticus

1–7	179

Numbers
- 11:29 79
- 24:17 120
- 27:15–18 79

Deuteronomy
- 4:29 78
- 28:22 78
- 28:38–42 78
- 30:2–3 78
- 30:6 78
- 30:6–8 39
- 31:16–22 65

Joshua
- 1:16–17 24

Judges
- 14:5–6 79

1 Samuel
- 16:1 117
- 16:13 117
- 16:14 79

2 Samuel
- 7:10–13 154
- 7:12–13 117

Psalms
- 2 .... 196, 197
- 23 .... 29, 194, 195
- 23:1–2 33
- 28:8–9 33
- 51:11 79
- 68:4 50
- 78:72 24
- 104:3–4 50
- 139:7–8 105

Isaiah
- 9:6 189
- 19:1 50
- 32:14–15 86
- 40:10–11 33
- 44:3 86
- 54:5–8 64
- 61:10 69

Jeremiah
- 2:2 64
- 7:3–11 78
- 17:9 38

Ezekiel
- 12:3–6 38
- 16:8–21 64
- 34 28
- 34:2–4 25
- 34:7–10 24
- 34:7–16 .... 19, 21, 22, 23, 24, 28, 30
- 34:11 33
- 34:11–16 24
- 34:16 25
- 34:23–24 25
- 36:26 43
- 36:27 43
- 36:26–27 .... 35, 36, 37, 38, 44
- 39:29 87

Daniel
- 7 .... 50, 51, 54, 55
- 7:1–8 50
- 7:9–10 50
- 7:11–12 50
- 7:13 50
- 7:13–14 .... 47, 48, 49, 50, 51, 54, 55, 56
- 7:14 50

7:15	50
7:17	50

Hosea

1:2	64
1:2–3	59, 61, 62, 64, 68, 70
1:11	189
2:19	73
3:1	65
3:1–5	59, 61, 63, 64, 68, 70
3:4–5	65
14:4–7	65

Joel

1:1	78
1:1–2:27	76
1:2–4	78
1:13–20	78
1:15	78
2:1	78
2:11	78
2:12–13	78
2:12–17	78
2:13	79
2:18–27	79
2:28–29	75, 76, 77, 80, 82, 84, 86, 87
2:28–32	78, 79
2:31	78
2:32	83
3:14	78

Amos

2:4–8	92
3:10	92
4:9	92
4:11	92
9	92
9:7–10	92

9:11	90, 93
9:11–12	89, 91, 92, 93, 96, 97, 98
9:11–15	92
9:12	90, 93
9:13–15	93

Jonah

1	104, 108, 109
1:3	104
1:9	104, 105
1:17	101, 102, 103, 106, 108, 110
3:10–4:2	109
4:1–2	104

Micah

1:2–7	116
1:4	116, 117
1:5	116
4:1–2	116
4:5	117
4:5–7	116
4:6	117
4:7	117
5:2	113, 114, 115, 118, 120, 121, 179
5:2–4	120, 122
5:2–6	116
5:3–6	114
5:4	117, 121

Habakkuk

1:1–11	128
1:2	128
1:5–11	126
1:12–2:1	128
1:13	128, 129, 132
2:1	129
2:2	129
2:2–20	129

Index / 209

    2:4 .... 125, 126, 127, 128, 129, 132, 134
    2:6 128
    2:16 132
    3:13 129
    3:17–19 134

Zechariah
    1:3–4 140
    9:9 .... 137, 138, 139, 141, 144, 146, 149
    9:10 141
    9:9–12 .... 140, 144
    11:12–13 149
    12:10 149
    13:7 149

Malachi
    1:11–13 154
    2:1–9 154
    2:14 154
    3:1 .... 152, 159
    3:1–5 .... 151, 152, 153, 154, 158, 160
    3:2–3 .... 152, 155
    3:5 155
    3:7 155

NEW TESTAMENT

Matthew
    1:1 121
    2 120
    2:1–2 120
    2:1–6 179
    2:3 120
    2:4–6 .... 113, 118, 119, 120, 122
    2:6 .... 33, 121
    4:1–11 179
    8:20 55
    12:38 108
    12:38–41 108

12:40 .... 101, 106, 107, 110
18:10–14 29
21:1–11 149
23:4 28
24:29–31 .... 47, 52, 53, 54, 55, 56
24:30 .... 52, 55
24:31 52
24:39 55
24:42–44 55
26:15 149
26:31 149
26:56 149
26:63–64 55
26:64 55
27:3–10 149
28:19 98

Mark
10:45 55
11:14 158
11:15 156
11:15–18 .... 151, 156, 157, 158, 160
11:17 .... 156, 158
11:18 156
11:27–33 159

Luke
2:4 121
5:31–32 108
24:44–47 178
24:46–49 82

John
1:14 108
1:29 171
5:39 178
10 28
10:11 .... 33, 121

Index / 211

10:11–15	19, 26, 27, 28, 29, 30
10:14	29
10:16	30
10:17–18	28
10:27	30
10:28–29	29, 30
12	144
12:12–16	137, 142, 143, 144, 145, 146, 149
12:13	142, 144
12:16	142, 144
15:26	83
16:7–8	83
16:8	85
19:34–37	149

Acts

1:1	84
1:2–3	82
1:4–8	82
1:8	82
1:9–11	55
2	75
2:1–11	80, 82
2:13	82
2:14–21	87
2:21	83
2:32–33	75, 80, 81, 82, 84, 86
2:33	80, 83, 87
2:38–39	83, 84
13:46–48	96
15	97
15:1–5	96
15:7–11	96
15:15–19	89, 94, 95, 96, 98
15:16	94
15:16–19	94
15:17	94
15:19	94

Romans
- 1:16 ... 130, 134
- 1:16–17 ... 125, 130, 131, 132, 133, 134, 135
- 1:17 ... 133
- 3:22–24 ... 132
- 8:1 ... 40
- 8:1–2 ... 42
- 8:1–4 ... 35, 40, 41, 42, 44
- 8:1–13 ... 84
- 8:3–4 ... 42
- 8:9 ... 83, 87
- 8:14–17 ... 85
- 8:19 ... 171

1 Corinthians
- 12:3 ... 87
- 12:13 ... 83, 87
- 15:42–49 ... 160
- 15:49 ... 69
- 15:51–53 ... 160

2 Corinthians
- 5:21 ... 69, 200–201

Galatians
- 3:10–14 ... 83
- 3:11 ... 132
- 3:13 ... 172
- 3:24 ... 42
- 5:22–24 ... 44
- 5:22–25 ... 43

Ephesians
- 1:14 44
- 2:11–15 97
- 4:30 69
- 4:32 71
- 5:25–32 .... 59, 66, 67, 68, 70
- 5:27 69
- 5:29–31 69
- 5:31 68
- 5:32 68

Philippians
- 1:6 70
- 2:5–8 .... 109, 144
- 2:6 144
- 2:9–11 145
- 2:10–11 145

1 Timothy
- 2:3–4 98

2 Timothy
- 3:16 178

James
- 2:18 44

1 Peter
- 1:18–19 198
- 2:24–25 29

Revelation
- 1:7 55
- 7:9 145
- 7:17 .... 30, 33
- 11:15 145
- 19:7–8 69
- 21 .... 160, 168
- 21:1–7 170

21:6	170
22:1	171
22:1–3	163, 167, 168, 169, 170, 172
22:3	121, 171
22:20	171

Thank you for studying
God's Word with us!

CONNECT WITH US
@thedailygraceco
@dailygracepodcast

CONTACT US
info@thedailygraceco.com

SHARE
#thedailygraceco

VISIT US ONLINE
www.thedailygraceco.com

MORE DAILY GRACE
Daily Grace® Podcast